KV-027-486

From an original Water Colour by the late J. W. Bone.

GIBRALTAR COTTAGES, WINCHMORE HILL

The Telephone Exchange was erected on the site in 1937

MEMORIES OF WINCHMORE HILL

by

HORACE G. REGNART, M.A.

⊙

Printed and published by
MEYERS, BROOKS & CO., LTD.,
Silver Street, Enfield
1952

FOREWORD

I HAVE been asked to write an account of Winchmore Hill as it was sixty and seventy years ago, when it was a village in the midst of fields. I lived in Winchmore Hill from 1878 to 1948. Mr. Walker and Mr. Alfred Nottage very kindly reminded me of several names I had forgotten.

I had hoped that the late Mr. Tom Mason would also have assisted by correcting any errors in the proofs, for his knowledge of the district was profound. Unfortunately he died before the proofs were available.

The illustrations are from blocks lent to me by the printers, Messrs. Meyers, Brooks and Co., Ltd., of Enfield, and I am grateful to them for their kindness.

HORACE G. REGNART.

St. Helens,
    Crosshaven,
        Co. Cork.

September, 1952.

CONTENTS

ILLUSTRATIONS

CHAPTER I

THE VILLAGE

ONE day in March 1878, a little boy three years of age dressed in girls' clothes emerged from the station at Winchmore Hill accompanied by his nurse. The little boy was myself. At that time little boys did wear girls' clothes; earlier in the century they wore them till they went to Eton. Winchmore Hill in those days was a rural village in the midst of fields.

The houses on Manor House hill were the last bit of London. On the site of the dog racing track was a tile kiln—then came open country with green fields all the way to Wood Green. The road itself was a country road with grass verges on either side which might have been miles away from any town. On the left you came to a high stone gateway which had been the entrance to Harringay Park—a quarter of a century earlier this had been the home of a herd of pedigree Shorthorns. The house had been pulled down, and the land was obviously waiting for the builder. A little further on was a milestone set in the grass verge on the side of the road. I once saw a haystack on fire close to the railway where it crosses the road. Then came Wood Green, a straggling place extending from the commencement of the green now converted into gardens, to the "Nightingale." Near the Turnpike Lane turning were a few small Early Victorian villas. Some time about 1882 I saw the meet of a pack of hounds with all the hunting people mounted on their horses and dressed in pink, close to Wood Green Station. The Fishmongers Almshouses at the top of Jolly Butchers Hill were there. On the right the present Town Hall was a private residence with spacious grounds—further on was a similar one. Then came green fields all the way to the "Cock." On the left there were green fields all the way till we came to a wooden fence, the

The Cock Inn and Dead Man's Bridge.

boundary of Alderman Sidney's Bowes Manor Estate.
Here the trees on either side of the road met overhead.
Bowes Manor had been the residence of Lord Truro who
was Lord Chancellor. He married a daughter of the Duke
of Sussex, a son of George III who had married outside
the Royal Marriage Act, but members of the Royal Family
came to see them. On the Bowes Road side of the
property was a large barn. The "Cock" was a small
country inn. Then came a nursery. You then crossed
the brook by a very narrow bridge, and the New River
by a somewhat wider bridge. At the top of the Hill was
Truro House. Then you got green fields all the way to the
Triangle. On the left there were green fields all the way
with the railway line running through them. Past the
Triangle the trees again met overhead as far as the "Fox,"
another old country inn. On the right was The Lodge
which later on was the residence of Mr. Argenti. Then
came a delightful thatched cottage which was occupied by
Mr. Taylor's gardener. On the left was an estate of Mr.
Taylor's which was bounded by Aldermans Hill, Green
Lanes, and Fox Lane. Just beyond the railway station on
Aldermans Hill was a tall arched gateway which used to
be the entrance. Some years before Mr. Taylor had bought
the estate and had pulled down the Mansion as it was
said because he could not bear to see another man's
chimneys from his windows at Grovelands. Opposite the
"Fox" was Hazelwood Lane. At the junction into Green
Lanes there was a Post Office and then three or four
cottages, but the whole aspect was truly rural. Down the
lane there had been another herd of pedigree Shorthorns.
A few years earlier Mr. John Thornton, the pedigree
cattle auctioneer, had dispersed them and the sale is
recorded in Thornton's Circular. Continuing on the right
we came to one or two houses, and then came Hazelwood
House, the residence of Mr. Charles Morgan, whose father
used to race greyhounds and won the Waterloo Cup. The
estate was bounded on the other side by Hedge Lane. On
the left between the "Fox" and the site of St. John's

The Post Office, Palmers Green.

Church were half-a-dozen villas—the rest have been built since. Mr. Moore had one of them for a school. Before I went to a boarding school at Hampstead I went to Mr. Moore's in the morning for one term. For the first week or two Mrs. Moore took me by myself in their dining room, after that I joined the other boys. One of the boys was Butson, from Rowantree House. He was 16, I was 8. Another big boy was Read, who lived in 545 Green Lanes, one of the pair of tall white houses just past the junction of Hoppers Road. I bought a rabbit from him. Later on Mr. Moore moved his school to Glenwood House in Wades Hill. Beyond Hedge Lane on the right were more fields and the road was still a country road. About on the site of Greenwood Gardens was Oak Tree Villa, the residence of Pawnbroker Smith—he was a pawnbroker and was always referred to as Pop Smith to distinguish him from Gentleman Smith, otherwise Mr. Booth Smith, who lived in Hedge Lane. Then there was nothing more till we came to The Cedars, the residence of Mr. Purvis. The Metropolitan Water Board's pumping station had not been put up then. Mr. Purvis left some money to St. Paul's Church. Then on the site of Duncan Court was Highfield Grange, an old red brick house. The house had been a workhouse, and later a medical home. Charles Lamb and his sister Mary lived at different times both in Enfield and Edmonton. Mary was liable to temporary fits of insanity and when these were coming on her brother used to take her to Highfield Grange. At the time with which I am dealing it was the residence of Mr. Houlder, who was a solicitor and clerk to the Edmonton Local Board—until the year 1881 Winchmore Hill and Southgate were portions of the parish of Edmonton. There was a beautiful garden at the back which stretched down to the New River. I spent many happy hours with the Houlders; their sons were about my own age. My first children's party was at their house. They left the district about 1892. On the left-hand side at the junction of Hoppers Road was Avondale, the residence of Mr. William Walker, a cousin of

Alfred Walker, who built Stone Hall. Beyond this were the two tall white houses now numbered 545 and 547; then came a piece of derelict land which we used to call Eaton Park, it was a favourite camping place for gipsies. Part of the soil was sand and one of our governesses used to go there to get sand to put in her canary's cage—Stonard Road was the first road to be made on it and two houses were built on it and these remained the only two houses for many years. Then came a black tarred fence, the boundary of Highfield Park which extended as far as Compton Road. What is now the Broadway had fields on either side with trees meeting overhead. On the site of the Westminster Bank stood Fords Grove, the residence of Mr. Thomas Teshmaker Busk. He was a considerable landowner in the district. The Busks acquired the property through intermarriage with a Teshmaker—the Teshmakers were related to the Marquis of Crewe. Like Mr. William Walker, Mr. Busk was independent. The brick wall which bounded the Fords Grove Estate and a tarred fence which constituted the boundary of the Beaulieu Estate which was the residence of Mr. Phillips, filled up the space till we arrived at the "Green Dragon. On the opposite side of the road there was a row of wooden cottages which were the property of Mr. Busk. Bush, his cowman, lived in one. Close to the cottages and opposite to Elm Park Road was an old house "The Shrubbery," first the residence of Mr. Warner, then of Mr. Gurlit and then of the late Colonel Willis, before he moved into Elm Park Road. The rest of the road was bordered by fields.

In the bend of the road is the "Green Dragon." It was then quite a small inn. The architecture was Georgian. It had a porch with imitation marble pillars. Adjoining it was a long open shed with a manger in which to tie up the patrons' horses. A picture of a green dragon was painted on the roof. On a fine Sunday evening in the summer we used to see a constant stream of smart gigs and dogcarts all making for the "Green Dragon" or some similar establishment further afield. Most of the inns in

Green Lanes had similar accommodation for horses, and if you drove along the road on a fine summer's evening you saw all the sheds pretty well filled, which shows that Green Lanes was a favourite drive. The "Green Dragon" stood originally at the corner of Green Dragon Lane. About 1780 a highwayman was hanged in front of it as being near the scene of his crime. It was moved to its present position soon after.

Towards the end of the eighties steam trams were put on from Finsbury Park to the foot of Jolly Butcher's Hill. Subsequently horse trams were substituted for them, and then eventually the trolleybuses were put on to run to Enfield.

CHAPTER II

HARRY COX

IN his Recollections which were published when he was ninety years of age and domiciled in Australia, Harry Cox tells us a good deal about Winchmore Hill in the forties and early fifties of the last century. He tells us he was born in 1839 in the road which runs from Green Lanes to the Worlds End, and that the buildings of Swain's Farm were opposite their cottage—it was evidently in Green Dragon Lane, somewhere near the junction with Wades Hill—and has evidently been demolished and the ground thrown into either the Chase or Eversley Park. He tells us that his father was confidential man to Mr. John Wade. He also tells us that Mr. Wade kept many cattle and that his father used to act as arbitrator between Mr. Wade and the men who mowed the grass. We can therefore put him down as the bailiff of the estate.

When Cox was three-and-a-half, that will be in May 1843, the family moved to Jessamine Cottage in Vicarsmoor Lane. They got their drinking water from a well in the garden but when they wanted a larger quantity for washing, etc., they had to fetch it from the Vicar's Well next to Pritchett Terrace. If they wanted the water brought to them they had to pay one shilling for 50 gallons—if they fetched it themselves they paid nothing.

He tells us the district was divided into fields of about 10 acres but only a few had gentlemen's houses on them. There were also about half-a-dozen gentlemen's houses with no land attached and about a dozen houses where retired people lived, with only one servant and an occasional man or boy to help. Some three or four wealthy London merchants had two or more of these fields and went up to London every day. John Wade was a merchant tailor. He was supposed to be the richest man in Winchmore Hill. He lived in Beaumont Lodge in what was afterwards named Wades Hill. It was the largest house in the place. He also had most land, the most livestock, the largest lawns and the largest flower and fruit gardens. He was very pompous, his wife was the only lady who had a page to follow her to church to open the door of the pew for her and to arrange her cushions and hassock. The doors of the pews were there in my day. The wife drove a very smart pony and trap. The houseman groomed the pony and his father, Cox senior, fed it. The houseman also cleaned the carriage. The Wades were ridiculed because they were not real gentry. Some little way from the Cox's cottage was Beadle's furniture store. Harry Cox was standing admiring the furniture in the windows when he was nearly run over by a four-horse coach that ran every day from Southgate to Bishopsgate, taking the City gentlemen to their businesses. The traffic to the City went along the main road through Edmonton and Tottenham. The nearest way was down Middle Lane which is now known as Station Road and Fords Grove—but there were no houses there so the coach evidently went down Vicars-moor Lane in order to pick up passengers.

Harry tells us he went to school down Church Hill. There are three wooden cottages. The middle one has only a single storey. This was the village school before what we know as St. Paul's School was built in 1858. He tells us he had to go up six steps to reach the door—actually there are only five. Mrs. Newman was the teacher. Her husband was confidential man to Mr. Mann of Rose-neath—like his father was to Mr. Wade. The school was attached to St. Paul's Church and he tells us how all the boys were taken to church every Sunday and sat in the Gallery at the West end of the Church as they do today. Cox's father, however, was a strong nonconformist and was trustee of the Congregational Chapel which then stood in Hoppers Road between the end of Holly Lodge garden and the Skew bridge. It was pulled down when the railway line was made and a new chapel was built in the Back Lane which is now called Compton Road.

B

He tells us how he tried to learn and to beat the other boys. Eventually he left the Winchmore Hill School and went to the Congregational Boys' School in Chase Side, Enfield. He says the walk to Enfield was one-and-a-half miles through fields and half-a-mile along the bank of the New River—you took the footpath that led from Vicars-moor Lane to Green Dragon Lane. You crossed Green Dragon Lane and took another footpath that ran through Pikes Farm. You crossed Salmons Brook by a wooden bridge. The path then went up to the top of the hill where you crossed a lane, you then took a footpath that led you down on to the bank of the New River. You went along passing the Twells estate which is now Enfield's Public Park on your right and you entered Enfield at the foot of Windmill Hill. Before the builders came this was the way everybody walked to Enfield.

When they wanted to buy flour they went to the windmill at Edmonton. They were driven to Hyde Park to see the 1851 Exhibition by Newby who had a livery stable on Wades Hill on the site of Burleigh Terrace— Police-Sergeant Hannon lived next to them at Iver. Cox tells us how Hannon was stabbed but not fatally by another policeman he caught milking Risley's cows.

When he was 13 he went to work in a grocery business in Kingsland and lodged with one of Thomas' employees named Burton. He emigrated to Australia in 1859. He settled on some land near Minyip in 1875, he became Chairman of the Wimmera United Waterworks Trust, 1894. He died in 1935 at the age of 96 years.

It is unfortunate that Cox does not tell us more about the people. He naturally mentions his father's employer. He also mentions Mr. Mann of Roseneath and also Newman and his wife. He also tells us about Mr. Cole, a gentleman who lived near Cock Hill, now Eversley Park Road—and whose wife drove a carriage. He also mentions Mr. Thomas Henry, whose name appears in the 1859 direc-tory—he also mentions Ball, the organist and choirmaster at St. Paul's, but he does not mention the Vicar.

He mentions Mrs. Catchpool, a Quaker lady, but does not mention Miss Creswell's grandmother who lived almost next door to them, nor does he even mention the doctor; he only mentions the "King's Head," he says every road leads uphill to it, which is perfectly true and the "Green Dragon" and the "Cock." He does, however, mention a beer shop between Colney Hatch and Southgate that has obviously been done away with.

CHAPTER III

1859 DIRECTORY

THE Post Office Directory for the year 1859 is very interesting. It gives the population of Winchmore Hill as 2,000. The living of St. Paul's was worth £100 a year. An omnibus left the "King's Head" for Enfield on week days at 8.45 a.m. and 2 and 5.45 p.m. On Sundays at 9 and 10 a.m. and 7.30 p.m. Letters were collected four times a day and there were also four deliveries, the last at 8 p.m. Letters came through Edmonton by foot post. The nearest money order office was at Southgate.

The directory gives the names of seventy-one private residents, in many cases their addresses are given too. Twenty-seven have esquire after their names. The rest are plain mister. Only nine of them had any representatives in Winchmore Hill at the time I was old enough to know the names of my neighbours, say in 1884. Today not a single one is left. There are 60 names in the commercial list, of these eleven had representatives in the place in my time, but only two of these, Beadle and Waters have any descendants here today. Some of them changed their businesses. In 1859 Riley was a plumber, a painter and a glazier. Later he became a grocer and had the Post Office. Mortiboy was a florist. In my day he owned a farm in Fords Grove and had a milk round which his son sold to Nix in 1896.

There were five people in Fords Grove, Thomas Busk, Matthew Costin, John Farrin, John Simmons and Lieutenant Tills. In my day there were only two, Busk and Mortiboy. I presume that Busk demolished the other three houses and added the sites to his own estate. All the present houses in Winchmore Hill Road from the Chase Side Tavern to Park House were in existence then. Ruskin Court is on the site of the Ivies. Mr. Leath lived in Winchmore Villa and his widow was there in my day.

St. Paul's School which had just been built is described as being in Chase Lane. It is true that Harry Cox, in his account of his recollections, calls it Church Hill, but he had been in correspondence with local people and evidently knew the name had been changed. Mrs. Newman who taught Harry Cox was still the mistress.

CHAPTER IV

THE RAILWAY

IN her book on Winchmore Hill, Miss Cresswell tells us how the railway from Wood Green to Enfield was opened in 1872. The trains were few. The last one down from King's Cross arrived at Winchmore Hill at 9.37 p.m. On Wednesdays and Fridays three coaches were attached to the 12.10 midnight train from King's Cross to Hatfield, were detached at Wood Green and brought to Enfield arriving at Winchmore Hill at 12.40 a.m. These were for the benefit of people who wished to go to the theatre.

The stations at Harringay, Bowes Park and Grange Park did not exist, but on the other hand there was a station at Holloway, entrance in the Holloway Road, which has been done away with. Only King's Cross and Finsbury Park had any waiting rooms. The platforms at Winchmore Hill have been lengthened—otherwise if you remove the waiting rooms and the roofs over the platforms you can see the station just as it was 76 years ago. I have a vivid recollection of the down platforms at Wood Green and Hornsey which were the counterparts of the platform at Winchmore Hill. On three occasions I can remember Grove Lodge being underpinned to prevent the house falling on to the platforms. When the line was made they pulled down the house of Mr. Morgan's father which stood in Vicarsmoor Lane, so they built Grove Lodge to take its place. The line has been widened out of all recognition. In the neighbourhood of Hornsey on the left going up to London there were some houses with very beautiful gardens with the New River running through them. They disappeared years ago. Going up, all tickets used to be collected at Holloway.

The South-Eastern Railway used to run trains on the Great Northern Line. Three trains a day used to run from Enfield to Victoria. I have a vivid recollection of the first station-master I knew at Winchmore Hill, an old man with a long white beard. He always used to speak to me and my nurse.

The Great Eastern Railway was the first one to issue cheap workmen's tickets with the result that Tottenham and Edmonton which used to be good residential districts became purely working-class and I saw the big red brick Georgian houses being pulled down.

CHAPTER V

THE GREEN

THE green is much smaller than it was in the old days. Then the roads were narrow with just room enough for two vehicles to pass one another and only one of them, the one running up from the railway station to Wades Hill, could boast of a footpath, and a narrow one at that. That part of the green which is now a garden was a large pond on which the boys and youths used to slide when it was frozen over. Opposite Roseville was a slope by which vehicles could enter the pond and the tradespeople used to wash their carts in it. The other end of the green reached much nearer to the "King's Head" than it does now as there was only the narrow road in between. Here was a signpost showing the way to London, Edmonton, Enfield, Southgate and Potters Bar. At one corner of the pond section opposite to Guys shop was a pump. New River water was only laid on to the larger houses and the people in the others were dependent on wells. We used to see many people from round the green with pails and cans to fetch their water. The pump was put in by Mrs. Todd of Uplands and replaced the old well. There was no street lighting. Some time later I remember seeing the lamposts lying on the ground prior to being erected.

The area of the green has been curtailed twice in my time. On the first occasion they widened the road and the existing footpath—they also made a gravel footpath along the side of the green from the signpost by the "King's Head" to the junction of the road with the Hoppers Road. Another footpath was made across it to give the occupants of the Limes a short cut to the station, and willows were planted round the pond, of which only one now remains. A good slice was taken off the green and posts and rails were put round it. On the second occasion the roads were

The King's Head.

widened still further and the present wide pavements
replaced the two narrow footpaths—the pond was filled in,
the willow trees, with one exception, were cut down and the
present garden laid out.

In the old days the green occupied a more important
place in the life of the village than it does today. It was
where the boys used to play cricket. In the summer
months we saw them playing continually. Miss Cresswell
has told us how an itinerant photographer set up on the
green and took portraits. During one summer in the late
eighties an American named Sequah paid several visits to
the green. The object of his coming was to sell bottles
of liniment or something. As an advertisement he pulled
out teeth free of charge. You mounted up on to a waggon
which served as a platform in full view of everybody.
You sat down on a chair and he pulled out your tooth.
A brass band which he brought with him provided music
to cheer you up. A good many people had their teeth out.
During one summer in the late nineties a brass band from
Enfield used to come and play on the green on one evening
in the week. Mr. Morgan and I frequently went to listen
to it. In the opening years of this century Mr. James
Branch put up as the Radical candidate for the Enfield
Parliamentary Division of which Winchmore Hill at the
time formed part. He used to hold his meetings on the
green speaking from a carriage in which he had driven
here. He used to say Winchmore Hill was hopeless. His
audience were practically all Conservatives who always
heckled him severely. On one occasion he put up Mr.
Gainsford Smith from New Southgate to speak for him.
Mr. Gainsford Smith was a rabid teetotaller. He said
Winchmore Hill had three enemies, Messrs. Mann. Cross-
man and Paulin. Now Mr. Mann and Mr. Paulin had
lived in Winchmore Hill all their lives and were very much
liked. This led to a rumpus in which I expect I took
part. Mr. Branch was unable to get any further hearing
and drove away.

There used to be a large rookery in the trees in the

The pond on the Green.

grounds of Roseville. It added to the rural character of the village, but alas the rooks went off some years ago and set up a new home elsewhere. Otherwise Roseville has not changed. Mr. Ashley who was the general manager of the Great Northern Railway lived there. He afterwards built Vicarsmoor in Vicarsmoor Lane but he died before it was ready for his occupation. His son went about with Frank Cresswell, the son of our doctor. They both rode high bicycles—"penny-farthings." Ashley went to Cambridge and Cresswell told me how on one occasion they rode there together on their bicycles when Ashley was returning there for the beginning of term. After the Ashleys came the Pellatts. Miss Pellatt used to teach in the Sunday School and every Christmas Mr. Pellatt used to give a sheep for the poor of the parish. Next came Dr. Vivian who came here from Southgate. Adjoining Roseville was the garden belonging to the old wooden shop in the Hoppers Road now belonging to Mr. Chalkley.

The little shop on the opposite corner that was Tidey's and is now the Dicky Bird was kept by the two Miss Hawkes. It was a sort of general shop for ladies' requirements, needles, cotton, etc. Our governess often used to be buying things there. They also sold children's toys. They had too a very diminutive circulating library. The bookcase was in a tiny alcove opposite the counter. It measured twenty-six inches wide. Of course the shelves went from the floor up to the ceiling, but the selection, of course, was not very great. When either of the Miss Hawkes showed you a book they read out the first couple of lines to you. I remember one book began "In Winchmore Hill there are as many thieves as there are blackberries." Both the sisters were very diminutive women and one was very deaf. They both addressed each other in the shop as "dear." They were both still going when I was quite grown up. The next shop was kept by a hunchbacked tailor named Critchlow. He made all my clothes till I went to a public school.

The old wooden shop now Stevens was kept by Mr

Riley, who is mentioned by Miss Cresswell in her book. In my time he was dead and his daughter kept it. It was a grocer's combined with the post office. We bought all our groceries there. There was one postman, Dan Harlow —his son ran a cab. Harlow was an old man with a white beard. We shared one telegraph boy with Edmonton. One day he would be in Edmonton in the morning and in Winchmore Hill in the afternoon. The next day it was vice versa, Winchmore Hill in the morning and Edmonton in the afternoon. In about 1879 or 1880 the present post office and shop was built on the garden belonging to the "King's Head," and Miss Riley transferred her business there. Her old shop was taken by Ironsides of Fulham, likewise a firm of grocers who ran it as a branch shop under Harris the manager, who became a well-known figure in Winchmore Hill. After many years Ironsides transferred the business to the shop now occupied by King on the other side of the green and eventually sold the business to Buckle. When Ironsides vacated the wooden shop it was taken by Aldridge the greengrocer, who moved from the small shop in the cul-de-sac now part of the Broad Walk. Between the shop and Mably's was a row of wooden cottages which stood well back from the road with long gardens in front. Some twenty-five years ago they were pulled down and Maynard's shop was built on the site. They were one of the last relics of the old village. Miss Knight painted a picture of them which I gave to the Borough Council. It is presumably in the museum in Broomfield Park. The draper's was kept by Miss Baker. Originally it had been her father's. I was often in the shop. The interior is just as it was 70 years ago. Miss Baker was followed by Richards and then came Mably.

Rowantree House has a history attached to it. In the early years of the nineteenth century Mr. Percival, the Prime Minister, was shot in the House of Commons by someone who had lost some money and imagined that his loss was the result of the policy of the Government. The son of the murderer took his mother's name and came to

live in this house. After some years he committed suicide.
The Greenshields were living here just about the time I
came to Winchmore Hill. When I was at Trinity Mrs.
Greenshields and her family were living in Cambridge
and the son was at the University. Mr. Drought, our
vicar, introduced me and I saw a good deal of them.
Some years ago Colonel Willis met the son, a vicar somewhere in Yorkshire. Butson then came to live here. He
was a builder and built Compton Terrace in Hoppers
Road. He divided the house into two as it is now. His
son was at Moore's School with me.

The beginning of what is now the Broad Walk was
a cul-de-sac leading up to the footpath through Taylor's
woods, the other end of which came out on the Bourne.
The first building on the right was Udall's shop. The shop
backed on to the cul-de-sac. The front looked out on a
garden with a lawn. In the garden were two stone figures
of lions. You went through the garden, the gate of which
opened on to a small extension of the green and was at
right angles to the cul-de-sac. Halfway up the garden the
door of the shop was on the left. Inside was a long
apartment with a counter running the whole length, behind
which were a row of shelves on which I remember seeing
rolls of cloth. One of the Bonners was the assistant. In
his history of the Congregational Church the Rev. W. A.
Oyler-Waterhouse says: In the old days Udall's was a
shop which dealt partly in foreign laces and silks, in
French gloves and Schnapps, in tea and brandy which
were brought by smugglers on pack-horses across the
treacherous marshes of Essex and Hackney and over the
Vicars moor and unloaded in the dark depths of Enfield
Chase, then almost surrounding Winchmore Hill. It was
a wild and lawless land in those days and haunted by
witches and hags and black bulls, and on the Wades Hill
side was known as Hagsditch. So cut off was Winchmore
Hill that even the revenue officers were unable to stop the
contraband traffic although they tried several times and
Udall's felt so safe that the stuff could be sold over the

Udall's Shop.

counter. It is a strange comment on those days to learn
that Udall's smugglers' shop was responsible for establish-
ing a little street chapel in Vicarsmoor Lane, although in
those days only Udallites attended it, today, of course,
it is very orthodox. But the Udallites who built it must
have been a queer lot. The minister was an old man living
in Middle Lane (now Station Road), and one Sunday he
was missing from chapel and when the Deacons went and
looked for him they found him hoeing potatoes. He had
forgotten it was Sunday. Later on, of course, the business
became quite respectable and did a roaring trade. People
used to tell of long strings of carriages waiting for the
customers they had brought from far and near. In my
time the shop belonged to Mrs. Childs, the last of the
Udalls. I often saw her as my nurse often took me with
her into the shop. She was an old lady with white hair
who wore a lace cap and a white shawl, but she soon
afterwards joined the majority and Mummery took the
shop for furniture. Next door was a small shop run by
Aldridge the greengrocer. Later on, when he had moved
to the wooden shop that Ironsides had vacated, Downes
took it as a corn merchants. Downes was born in a
cottage that stood on the site of the railway bridge on
Bourne Hill. Subsequently he took over Gabriel's shop
on the green. Then came half a dozen cottages known as
Woodside Cottages. On their site used to be a chapel.
Mr. Waterhouse tells us that when the chapel was pulled
down and the foundations prepared for the cottages a
surprising number of bones were found of persons who
had been buried in or near it, and which dated from about
1750. On the left-hand side of the cul-de-sac was a field.

The Limes today is just as it was 70 years ago. The
Horsmans lived there. Mr. Horsman's uncle was a wealthy
man who ran racehorses. He won the Derby with Blair
Athol. They had two daughters, one of whom unfortunately died when she was in the early twenties. The
son, Geoffrey, was a good deal younger than me. They
left about the end of the nineties and went to live near

Newbury. The Uplands, which stood on the site of Uplands Court, was an old, brown, brick Georgian house. A high, brick wall along Church Hill, which bounded the garden, extended to a point nearly opposite the Quakers. Mr. Botterall, a solicitor, lived there. His three sons, all much younger than me, all eventually went to Harrow.

Church Hill and Wades Hill were the boundaries of Enfield Chase. The Winchmore Hill Road used to be called Chase Side—there is the "Chase Side Tavern." Mr. Sewell's property on Wades Hill was called the Chase. Southgate was the southern gate of the Chase. The "King's Head" may, therefore, be said to be on the southern extremity of the Chase—Frank Cresswell told me he had seen the charter granted by King Edward I giving permission to hold a fair, since called Barnet Fair, at any spot between the "King's Head" at Winchmore Hill and some other tavern, the name and locality of which I forget. It was an old, brown brick, two-storied building with a porch with imitation marble pillars. In front was a low wooden fence on which they often used to put out the metal beer tankards. On the left of the porch was a fine wistaria. The proprietor was Ballantine. The present building was put up in 1896 and was put back to allow for the widening of the roads.

The garden of the "King's Head" was across the road. All the shops from Strangwick's to Nix's were built on it. The post office was the first—the actual shop was only about half the size it is at present. I imagine the other half of the building was used as a store. About forty years ago it was let to a hairdresser. The postal counter was at first a semi-circular affair against the wall and opposite the entrance—I remember seeing Miss Riley many times perched up in it—I was too small to be able to reach it. On one boiling hot summer's day Miss Riley told me how cool I looked in my sailor suit and that she wished she could wear the same. Since then the postal counter has occupied almost every possible position in the shop. Miss Riley lived over it. The other shops which were built in

the garden of the "King's Head" were built rather later.
Then there were four old shops which had been built on
to the fronts of old houses. They are those now occupied
by Downes, the wool shop, the cafe and King's. In
Downes and the wool shop we can see the steps which
led to the doors of the houses. The wool shop used to be
Watkins the ironmonger. There used to be a passage at
the side, along which you took horses to be shod in the
forge at the back. King's shop had once been a school
run by Miss Tills, whose father, Captain Tills, had been in
the Battle of Trafalgar and had lived in Mortiboy's house
in Fords Grove. Then came some cottages with longish
gardens in front, and finally two small cottages which were
occupied by Dunklin the village cobbler. He used one
to live in and the other to work in. I have spent many
hours in his shop talking to him. Cobblers must have had
a special attraction for me because many years later I also
used to go in to talk to Wright on Church Hill.

Grove House was occupied by Dr. Cresswell. The
railway company had built the house for Mr. Morgan's
father to take the place of the one he had in Vicarsmoor
Lane on the site of the railway bridge, which, of course,
was pulled down when the railway was built. Dr. Cresswell belonged to a good, old family, the Cresswells, of
Cresswell in Northumberland. One member of the family
had been a judge. He came to Winchmore Hill in 1842
and died in 1892. He lived first of all in a house next to
the Congregational Chapel on the site of the Skew Bridge
in Hoppers Road—both were done away with when the
railway was built. He then went to Grove Lodge. He was
of medium height. His hair was on his shoulders. He
wore a ragged beard. He was by no means smart. His
eyesight was none too good. At first he used to walk on
his round to his patients. Then he rode an old-fashioned
tricycle with a wooden seat, with handles at the side for
steering and for putting on the brake. He used to ride
in a frock coat and wearing a silk hat. He was our family
doctor for many years. He was a good judge of pictures

and his chief interest in life was painting. He painted the local scenes. After his death his daughter gave a hundred of his pictures to the Southgate Borough Council. Before the war they were in the museum in Broomfield Park. Winchmore Hill has better record of what it was before it was built over than any other part of London possesses. Mrs. Cresswell died in 1886. Subsequently his brother-in-law, Mr. Willink, came to live with him. Dr. Cresswell had one son, Frank, who, like his father, became a doctor. He was a most interesting man to talk to as he had a wonderful accumulation of knowledge. He married a cousin, the daughter of the Vicar of Cottesmore. He built Cottesmore in Station Road and moved away into the country in 1906. The daughter, Henrietta Cresswell, was in the twenties when I first remember her. She wrote the book on Winchmore Hill to help a bazaar that was got up by Mr. Dewdney in 1903 or 1904 to raise some money to build Holy Trinity Church in the Broadway. The bazaar was held in Mr. Paulin's grounds at Broadfield. She wrote a second edition of the book which, however, she did not publish as she thought she had given too many personal details about the inhabitants. She was a good scholar. In church she used to follow the second lesson in the original Greek which the vicar, Mr. Drought, did not approve of. After her father's death she lived in Station Road in the house with the big cherry tree in the front garden. Then she went to live in Dumfries, where she died.

The Village Hall at the junction of Wilson Street and The Green was put up in 1887 to commemorate Queen Victoria's first jubilee. It was used for dances, etc. It was pulled down when Mr. Dewdney built St. Paul's Institute.

CHAPTER VI

GROVELANDS

GROVELANDS PARK used to be called Southgate Grove. The house, which is now a hospital, was built by Mr. Walker Gray in 1797. The architect was Nash. Mr. Gray's mother was a sister of Isaac Walker of Arnos Grove. The acreage of Southgate Grove was about 79 acres in a long narrow strip from the house to Church Hill. Mr. Gray also owned 109 acres of the Winchmore Hill woods which were then known as Gray's woods. Mr. Gray died about 1839 and the estate went to his nephew, John Vickris Taylor. The Taylors had been resident in Southgate for about 100 years. They lived in a house in Fox Lane near the eastern end of Selborne Road. They had an interest in the brewery firm of Taylor Walker. The firm was founded in 1730 as Harford and Taylor. In 1816 the Walkers of Arnos Grove acquired an interest in it and in 1843 the Taylors sold out their interest. Mr. Taylor could not bear to see another man's chimney from his windows. He therefore bought as much land as he could, pulled down the houses and threw the land into his estate. Half-way along Chase Side we used to see two cedar trees standing in the park a good distance from the road. These trees marked the site of a house Mr. Taylor had pulled down.

Except for Miss Barnes' property on Church Hill and a strip round the Green which included Uplands, the Limes and the shops and cottages, and another strip in Hoppers Road which extended as far as the cottages beyond the "Salisbury," the Grovelands Estate eventually extended from the present Southgate Circus, along Chase Side now called Winchmore Hill Road, Church Hill, Hoppers Road and the Bourne. It contained 314 acres. He also bought Cullands Grove and Bone Grove he inherited from his father. This gave him all the land between Aldermans Hill, Cannon Hill and Fox Lane extending from Green Lanes to the level of the "Woodman," eliminating the "Cherry Tree" and the neighbouring houses. Cullands Grove had been the property of Alderman Sir William Curtis after whom Aldermans Hill is named. He was a friend of George IV who often used to come to Cullands to dine with him. Old inhabitants of Southgate used to tell of the number of carriages that were put up at the "Cherry Tree" on these occasions. Mr. Taylor pulled down the houses and threw the land into his estate. He also bought the "Fox Inn," The Lodge Estate at the Triangle in Palmers Green, some land on the opposite side of Chase Side which constituted the Home Farm and some land in Waterfall Lane which extended up to New Southgate. Eventually the estate extended to 600 acres. He always refused to sell any land for building but he gave the land for the St. Paul's Schools in 1857. He fought extremely hard against the making of the railway through his land. Palmers Green Station was built on his land and it took a slice off his land the length of Hoppers Road to the skew bridge. For several years after Palmers Green Station was opened for traffic he ran a bus from Southgate to the City to compete against the railway. I often saw him. He was an old man who always wore a white tall hat. He died in 1885.

His son, Major Robert Kirkpatrick Taylor, of the Shropshire Light Infantry, succeeded to the property. He kept a herd of deer in the park. The family used to come up to Church every Sunday along a footpath through the park which led to the school yard. He had two sons and two daughters. Major Taylor and the elder girl used to come to the dances in the Village Hall in Southgate that were got up by the Southgate Tennis Club.

On Major Taylor's death, his son, Captain John Vickris Taylor, succeeded to the property and he put it up for sale in June 1902. Grovelands was bought in, the rest of the estate being sold, Captain Taylor finally left the district in 1906. In 1911 the District Council bought 64 acres as a public park.   Eventually another purchase increased this to 91 acres.   Captain Taylor lent the house in June 1916 to the Middlesex Voluntary Aid Detachment as a war hospital and in 1921 it was purchased by the Middlesex V.A.D. together with 6 acres of land, and given to the Royal Northern Hospital as a Convalescent Home. The remainder of the park was sold for building.   If the Taylors had not sold other estates the district would have retained its rural character to a large extent.

CHAPTER VII

THE WOOD

THE woods were the chief attraction for the inhabitants of Winchmore Hill. After Church on a Sunday you met many people walking through the wood. Our French governesses often took us there for our walk. We often met Miss Cresswell. We went up a cul-de-sac which is now part of Broad Walk and entered by a gate. There was a wide gravelled path which went all the way to Bourne Hill. First of all there was a field on each side and then came the wood proper. The right-hand side was fenced to ensure the privacy of the park of Grovelands. The other side was open and unspoilt woodland which stretched as far as Bourne Hill and Hoppers Road or the meadows on Hoppers Road. It was a primeval forest of oak and beech, fir and holly. The undergrowth was in many places very dense and there was much bracken. On the right about three-quarters of the way along was the Keeper's Cottage—Wakelin was the Keeper. Further along on the left were a few acres of grass which were not fenced. At the end of the path you got over a stile and were in Bourne Hill. Opposite the stile were some cottages. One day our dogs which we always took with us on our walks killed some fowls belonging to the people in one of the cottages and our French governess had a heated argument with their owner.

If you were going to Southgate you turned to the right as far as the junction with Fox Lane. Then you went a short distance down Fox Lane and crossed another stile into the Cherry Tree Fields. Here was a footpath which went out at the side of the "Cherry Tree Inn." These fields were originally part of Alderman Curtis' Cullands Grove Estate. King George IV often came to Cullands Grove to see his friend Curtis. The Taylors bought the estate and pulled down the mansion. Till

Path through the Wood past the Keeper's Cottage.

recently the gateway to the Grove, a stone arch, was to be seen in Aldermans Hill. There was a large pond in the fields and when it was frozen over we sometimes used to go there to skate and to slide.

Before the Weld Chapel in Southgate was built the Southgate people went to Edmonton Church. They crossed the Cherry Tree Fields, went through the wood, crossed Winchmore Hill green, went down Station Road and Fords Grove. Then they crossed Firs Lane and entered a footpath across a field which took them to the Hyde. They then turned to the right and about a mile further on was Edmonton Church. Walking funerals, which were pretty general in those days, also went this way.

Path through the Wood looking towards the Green.

CHAPTER VIII

HOPPERS ROAD

D RIVING home from London, Miss Cresswell used to
go into raptures over the beauties of Hoppers Road
—she says the scenery was enchanting. On the left
were pines and larches, beeches and oaks, old forest land
and the newer plantations, the unspoilt virgin woodland
of Enfield Chase. There were trees that were centuries
old and even the fields were full of fine timber. The
hedgerows were bowers of hawthorn, a perfect snowstorm
of bloom in Maytime. I knew it like that. On the left
from the Bourne to the brook in the dip the Winchmore
Hill woods came right up to the road. Then they receded
but we saw them in the distance beyond the railway line
and a field or two right up to the time we entered the
village. On the other side of the road, across the stream
in the dip, was a narrow field which extended to Green
Lanes. Beyond this was the boundary of Highfield Park,
which went right up to the foot of the skew bridge. It
was lined with chestnut trees, which, when they were in
bloom, were a sight. The entrance to the Park was
opposite the house; it consisted of a pair of iron gates and
an hexagonal thatched lodge—with a straight carriage-drive
up to the house. Formerly Captain Arlow, who was a
captain in the Life Guards, and whose wife was the
daughter of a peer, lived there. Arlow Road is called after
him. He was no relation to Mr. Arlow of Suburban

Houses past the Salisbury, Hoppers Road.

House. In my early days a man named Bartlett owned the estate. He had been a labourer on a farm, and he heard one day that a relative of his who had been lucky and had made money had left him the estate. He then came to live here. He farmed the land and it was said that he kept the manure in the dining room and the drawing room. He died in the early eighties when the estate was put up for sale. Mr. Mann went to the sale with the intention of buying it for his eldest son, but it fetched more than he was willing to give. The house, without the land, was then let to the Villiers who had formerly lived in Holly Cottage. They were followed by the Wilkinsons.

At the end of the road on the right, opposite Chalkley's shop, the premises which are now Graham's, was Wheeler's, who was a builder and used to do most of the repairs to the houses in the district. Then came Miss Light's, now Tidey's. We used to buy our sweets here. A fourteen-year-old girl used to serve in the shop. She wore her hair down her back. One day we met her on the green and our French governess asked her if the Magazine was open. Many years afterwards I met her again when she was an old woman and the second wife of Wright, the cobbler on Church Hill. And we had many talks about the village as it was in the old days. At one time Miss Light used to sell some round, flat sweets, a certain number of which had a sixpence inside so that if you were lucky you got your sweets for nothing, but eventually they had to be withdrawn as they contravened the gaming act. Miss Light was followed by Miss Knight.

The yard which is now Salters belonged originally to a wheelwright named Carpenter. In the early seventies Mr. Walker bought it. He used to build and repair all the tradesmen's carts and the carriages of the gentry which were quite numerous in the district. He lived at 2 Victoria Cottages and was one of the leading Liberals in the district. His son still occupies the house. He has been of great assistance to me in giving me the names of people who were going seventy years ago. Mrs. Stearns lived in the wooden cottage next to the yard. For many years she taught the infants in St. Paul's School. The butcher's shop and the Salisbury have both been moved further down the road in recent years. Nickels had the butcher's shop. The Holders had their meat from him, and his brother had a farm at Botany Bay, Enfield. Stockton bought the business some years ago. Then came the "Salisbury." Fred Press, who had been one of our grooms, became the owner through his marriage with the daughter of a former proprietor.

Opposite the junction with Compton Road was a very picturesque old red brick house, Belmont House, which was once a girls' school kept by Miss Tebb. Then came half a dozen cottages and finally Eaton's yard, quite a spacious place with several sheds in it. Eaton was uncle to the Eatons of Southgate. Eaton was one of the two carriers in Winchmore Hill. Press, the uncle of the Press in the shop in Middle Lane, was the other. Eventually Press was killed on the railway during shunting operations. Bunce and he used to drive up to London on so many days in the week taking up parcels, etc., and bringing back others. Beyond Eaton's yard was a field which extended to the skew bridge and went back to the boundary of the woods. It was occupied by Joe King, who was also the tenant of the home farm in Chase Side now known as Winchmore Hill Road. Our celebrations on the occasion of Queen Victoria's first jubilee in 1887 took place in this field. A meal was given to all the old people in the village and in the evening there were fireworks. On the other side of the bridge, fields extended all the way to Pellats Grove, a long, white stucco house, the garden of which extended as far as the brook in the dip. Behind the house were two large weeping willows which overhung the railway bank. There were also some disused pigsties; some of the previous occupiers had evidently kept pigs. Dr. Cresswell told us that in the fifties a Frenchman lived in the house who contracted cholera and that he attended him and cured him. In my day Mr. Bowhay had it as a school.

I had not been doing very well at my boarding school so I spent the twelve months before I went to Clifton at Bowhays. Arthur and Hugh Houlder, Charlie Page and Charlie Litchfield were the other Winchmore Hill boys who went there. There were also two Powers from Bush House, Southgate, and two sons of a farmer on Bourne Hill. Mr. Bowhay's sons and daughters also had their lessons with us. At the end of the twelve months I went up for the entrance examination into Clifton College. My mother and I put up at the Clifton Down Hotel, and I went every day to sit for the examination which was held in one of the lecture rooms. I passed in all right and on

our return home was taken to a tailor's in London to be
measured for my first pair of long trousers. I entered the
school in January, 1888.

Beyond the stream at the foot of Bowhay's garden
was a portion of the Winchmore Hill woods which
extended to the Bourne. Between the Bourne and Green
Lanes was another field. On the side of the road was a
pond which usually had some ducks on it.

On the other side of the road, at the Green end, was
Goldworthy's old wooden shop now Chalkley's. The
garden, which is now all built over, extended to the Green
and to Roseville. At the back were extensive outbuildings.
The site of what is now Compton Terrace was a field, with
a wooden barn with a red-tiled roof at the Compton Road
end. Opposite the "Salisbury" was the inn's signboard.

At the junction with Back Lane, now Compton Road,
was a triangle of grass with a fenced-in shrubbery of
hawthorns with a fine chestnut tree in the middle which
is still standing. Between here and the skew bridge was
a black-tarred fence, the boundary of Holly Lodge,
which is still standing as one of the relics of old Winchmore
Hill. Highfield Park has already been described. On the
rising ground beyond the dip was a large, red-brick house
standing in its own grounds and also named Highfield. It
was the property of Mr. Kelsey whose son, Frank, was at
Moore's school with me. Later on it became a girls' school
till the house was pulled down and the land developed.
Then came the row of cottages which are still standing,
but most of which have been turned into shops. Here was
also the "Dog and Duck," which has now been modernised.

The Dog and Duck, Hoppers Road.

D

In those days Stonard Road had not been made. A vacant piece of land, which was not fenced and which was known as Eaton Park, extended from Hoppers Road to Green Lanes, and also went behind the cottages and the "Dog and Duck." It was often frequented by gipsies who used to hawk their wares round the village. Then came Eaton Villa, an old red-brick house. In the days of the Southgate Poultry Show a successful breeder of Black Minorcas lived here. Then came Avondale, a house standing in its own grounds; a cedar tree is still standing. Mr. William Walker, a cousin of Alfred Walker who built Stone Hall, lived there. The property was bounded on the other side by Green Lanes.

CHAPTER IX

WADES HILL

WADES HILL was named after John Wade, whom
Harry Cox tells us so much about. On the right
was a brick wall which enclosed the garden of the
"King's Head." The shops have now been built on the site.
Then came the three houses. An elderly couple, Mr. and
Mrs. Foster, lived in the first one, No. 17. He was a retired
builder. They used to drive about in an old-fashioned
four-wheeled pony trap. Their daughter married Mr.
Dobbs who was the Municipal Surveyor for Edmonton.
They had one small boy. The Fosters had the pew in
front of ours in St. Paul's Church. Mr. and Mrs. Dobbs
and the grandson were always there with them. Next were
four cottages. Charlie Finch, who came on the committee
of the Conservative Association, lived in the first one.
Then came a small field. Later Mr. Walker, of Percy
Lodge, rented the field and made tennis courts. The
garden of Percy Lodge adjoined it. Percy Lodge is at
the corner of Wades Hill and Vicarsmoor Lane. Sharon
Turner, the historian, lived here. He was a friend of
Disraeli's father and arranged for Disraeli's admission
into the Church of England. Mr. and Mrs. Schofield lived
here for some time but then moved to Potters Bar and Mr.
William Walker followed them. He was no relation to
Alfred Walker of Stone Hall nor to William Walker of
Avondale. Percy Lodge has a beautiful garden and Mr.
Walker was a very keen gardener. They had several
sons and two daughters. They came to our dances and
I have been to dances at their houses.

On the opposite side of Vicarsmoor Lane was Beaumont Lodge where Mr. Wade lived. Then came fields
which belonged to the Chase. The house stood well back
from the road near the junction with Green Dragon Lane
which bounded the estate on that side. Mr. Sewell lived

Beaumont Lodge, Wades Hill.

here. He kept a herd of Kerry cows. He had one son and two daughters who were much older than me. The younger one married George Hatcher. I have been to dances at the house. Mr. Sewell left the district about 1910.

On the left-hand side Braids Nursery extended from the "King's Head" to Glenwood House. A house and a shop where Braid lived and did his business adjoined the "King's Head." There were several greenhouses, and a very thick holly hedge which was kept well trimmed was the boundary to the road. Miss Cresswell says the Pelargoniums, Chinese Primroses and Cinerarias were of great renown both in the village and in London and that he was a kind man who would always find a plant for a penny for some small person's garden. Glenwood House was semi-detached. Mr. Frost, the previous vicar, had lived here. Mr. Drought came to Winchmore Hill in 1874. With him were his mother, who died in 1888, his brother, Adolphus, and his two sisters, Sarah and Charlotte. They were Irish and came from Parsons Town. Mr. Drought took his Degree at Trinity College, Dublin. When Beadle had built the houses on the site of his burnt-out shop in Vicarsmoor Lane the Droughts moved to one of them and Mr. Moore who had the school in Palmers Green where I had been for a short time took it and had his school there for many years. The house adjoining was the Elms. This house was larger than Glenwood and whereas Glenwood had a small garden the Elms had a large one which extended as far as the boundary of Hill House, a hedge separating the two gardens. There were stables and Mr. Moxon who lived here kept several horses. He was for many years churchwarden of St. Paul's and he and Mr. Hope read the lessons. He had one daughter who was much older than I was and she married an officer in the Army. Subsequently his nephew was a fellow Liveryman of mine in the Merchant Taylors Company. When the Moxons left Mr. Adams from Woodbank, Chase Side, took the house.

Then came Burleigh Terrace. Mrs. Mudge lived in

the first house, now No. 52. She collected the pew rents
for Mr. Drought. Once when she came I was in the dining
room with my mother and she made me dive under the
dining table so that I should not be seen. Her daughter
wrote some novels and undertook the education of Mr.
Paulin's two daughters. Martin, who was Mr. Mann's
coachman, lived in the last one. He was always referred
to as Mr. Martin. A woman once asked her small son if
he had seen anyone when he was out and he said he had
seen Mr. Martin riding Tommy Mann's horse.

Then came the entrance to Broadfields where Mr.
Paulin lived. When he married Miss Mann he bought a
small farm and built the house. Beyond the entrance was
Memorial Terrace which consisted of a row of almshouses
for old women. The charity to which they belonged had
no connection with Winchmore Hill. There was also a
house for a caretaker and Beard who worked for Wheeler
and was also the verger at St. Paul's was the caretaker.
Then came the fields belonging to Broadfields which extended as far as the footpath to Church Hill. Standing
some little way from the road was a farmyard and farm
buildings. Mr. Paulin kept Jerseys. In the bottom of the
dip Hounsden gutter ran underneath the road and then
through Mr. Sewell's fields. Mr. Paulin had two daughters.
The elder one married Mr. Dewdney, who followed Mr.
Drought as vicar. Mr. Paulin did a tremendous lot for
the London Hospital and was subsequently knighted. He
died in 1931, when the land was sold for building.

Then came Eversley Park. Miss Cresswell tells us
that Mr. Wigan built the house in 1865 and that he dug
a well three hundred and fifty feet deep to get the water
for the house. The house was always called the Mansion.
The estate was bounded by Eversley Park Road, Green
Dragon Lane, Wades Hill, and the footpath from Wades
Hill to Church Hill, till the footpath crossed Hounsden
Gutter and then the gutter was the boundary. The main
entrance was at the top of Wades Hill with a secondary
entrance in Eversley Park Road. The stables were in

Green Dragon Lane. Mr. Wigan had two sons one of whom was subsequently created a baronet. The Wigans left about 1884. The house stood empty for some years when it was taken by Caroline, Marchioness of Ely, who lived there till her death, when the Wigans sold the land for building.

CHAPTER X

CHURCH HILL

D R. CRESSWELL told us that when he first came to
Winchmore Hill in 1842 Church Hill was only made
up as far as the Church and that beyond that it was
a grass road.

On the right-hand side a row of cottages adjoined
the "King's Head." Mr. Salmon the plumber lived in one
of them. A large black cat was usually to be seen sitting
in the window basking in the sun. When the shops were
built on the green he moved into one of them where his
son still carries on the business. When the "King's Head"
was rebuilt in 1896 it was put further back and the cottages
were done away with and a fire station was built adjoining
Devon House. Mr. Salmon was captain of the fire brigade.
Devon House and the adjoining butcher's shop belonged to
Mrs. Langley. We used to see her in the shop, an old
lady wearing a lace cap and a white shawl. Her son
served the customers. A window opened out of the dining
room in Devon House and her daughter used to sit there
to do the booking. All the meat was home killed. They
killed and dressed the meat in the covered yard at the
side of the shop and when the door was open passers-by
could see the operation. Subsequently a new slaughter
house was built at the back of the shop. Every morning
Langley used to stand his empty carts against the wall
on the opposite side of the road. This portion of the
road was very narrow and this made it very awkward for
the traffic. On his mother's death the son inherited the
business. In course of time he retired and sold it to a son
of Gocher, the butcher in Cheshunt. Then Potter had the
business and when he died Phillips took it and after a
few years moved the business to a shop in Wades Hill.
Then came the three cottages which are standing today.
In the centre one was Wright, the shoemaker, who for

Church Hill looking towards the Green.

many years made my boots and shoes. His second wife I
knew as the young girl who served in Light's shop in
Hoppers Road. We had many talks about the old days.
Some years ago Rat Hemmington went to live in the end
one. In his young days he was a noted runner and when
I was a boy I used to see him in his running gear doing
some practice runs. He died a few years ago, a very old
man. Then came some wooden cottages. A picture of
them is on the cover of the second edition of Miss Cresswell's book.

George Wicks, who was at one time our cowman,
lived in one of them. Mrs. Wicks was never seen without
a black straw hat. They used to say she slept in it.
They afterwards went to Southgate where Wicks was cowman to Sir Thomas Lipton. Then came a narrow cul-de-
sac with one row of cottages, one of which was the Penny
Bank. The Friends Meeting House is just as it always
has been except for the erection of the caretaker's house
a few years ago. The crescent-shaped ground in front of
the entrance is the Quakers' private property and one day
every year it is chained off to prevent the public getting
a right-of-way. The caretaker many years ago was an old
man named Storey. When the children came out of school
and passed by they sang, "Tell us the old, old story,"
which made him very wild. The Quakers have been dealt
with elsewhere.

We went to Hill House in 1878. The kitchen and
scullery were originally a pair of cottages. The tiled roof
which I had to replace a few years ago showed that they
were from four to five hundred years old. In the reign
of Queen Anne or soon after the house was added on to
them. George Patten, A.R.A., who was portrait painter
to the Prince Consort, was one of the people who lived
in the house. He died in 1865. When we went in there
was no water laid on, no gas, no bathroom and the sani-
tation was out of doors. On the lawn is a well, hidden
away by shrubs. All the occupiers previous to us got all
the water required for the house from this well. The

staircase went out of the dining room. Two of the windows in the back of the house were blocked up to escape the window tax. The stables were of tarred wood. My father had the water and gas laid on but we used oil lamps in the dining room and the drawing room. He also built the present staircase and put in the bathroom. He built the conservatory and the greenhouses and planted the vine. I had to rebuild them all. He also added two loose boxes to the stables.

Except that a slice has been taken from the orchard and added to the kitchen garden and that an oak fence has been substituted for a hedge on one side and a brick wall for a tarred wooden fence on the other side the garden and the orchard are exactly as they were when we went in. The monkey puzzle was then at its prime and the lowest branches touched the lawn. Half-way down the flower garden on the right was a big acacia tree. We had seats under it and there we often used to sit and sometimes have tea. There was a pigsty in the orchard which has been done away with. Miss Cresswell tells us how Mrs. Wadeson who was then living in the house asked her father to come and see her pigs as the old sow and all her young ones and all the poultry had been suddenly attacked with some mysterious illness. The explanation was quite simple. They were all tipsy. Neither the pigs nor the fowls could walk straight. There had been a great brewing of currant wine; the lees which were very alcoholic had been thrown out on the dung heap. The pigs and the poultry had eaten them and had evidently liked them. The old sow was as drunk as a lord. In a few days they had completely recovered. From the lawn we saw St. Mary's Church on the Ridgeway, Enfield, being built, and there was not a house in between. When you look up the yard and see the trees and the red-tiled roofs of the outbuildings you might be a hundred miles from London. Old Moore, as we children used to call him was the gardener. He lived in Highfield Row. He was soon followed by Clark, who came to us from Mr.

Walker of Arnos Grove. He came with us to Stone Hall where he was head gardener till 1895 when he retired owing to old age. James Barnes was coachman and he taught me to ride.

Mr. and Mrs. Richard Davies followed us into Hill House and were our friends for the rest of their lives. Later Mr. Davies went on to the Common Council in the City and was eventually knighted. The eldest son, Sidney, went to Oxford and entered the Church. The Kelseys followed the Davies.

On what is now the Laurel Lodge property there was what Miss Cresswell described as a cottage of gentility. Mr. Wright lived there. When we had been in Hill House a few months he died. About 1882 Mr. Mann bought the land and built the present house for his son who eventually became Sir Edward Mann, Baronet. He built the brick wall round the property. After his mother's death in the middle nineties, Sir Edward rebuilt his father's home, Roseneath, in Vicarsmoor Lane, and went to live there, but in a few years he left Winchmore Hill for good. Then Fred Barry, a son of Mr. Barry, of Bush Hill House, took Laurel Lodge and after a few years was followed by Mr Charles Morgan who came from Hazelwood House in Green Lanes. He died in the house in 1909.

Stone Hall was built in 1872 by Mr. Alfred Walker. He used stones of old Blackfriars Bridge to build the foundations and the walls of the cellars which extended to nearly the whole area of the house. When the new bridge was built an old lady was induced to buy the stones as a good investment. For many years they lay in a field in Wades Hill and eventually Mr. Walker bought them. Beaver Hall in Waterfall Lane, Southgate, had recently been pulled down by Mr. Walker of Arnos Grove in order to throw the land into his estate. Mr. Walker bought the doors, windows, mantelpieces, staircases, etc., in order to put them into the house he was going to build. He did his job well and when the rooms came to be pannelled and artistically decorated it was a very fine house. My father bought Stone Hall in 1885. The gardens were extensive but lacked the rural beauty which the garden at Hill House had. The trees in the belt along Church Hill were evidently planted many years before the house was built since some 70 years ago they were about the same size as they are now. In the dip at the bottom of Church Hill is a brook which runs under the road and was originally the boundary of the Stone Hall property. It eventually runs into the Hounsden Gutter. The brook is the overflow of the lake in Grovelands. One day in a flood the dam burst and our fields became flooded. Several fish were stranded on the grass in the fields and my mother had them cooked for breakfast. Eventually the Stone Hall property included Camelot and most of the land up to the boundary of Eversley Park. We had a herd of pedigree Jerseys. Towards the end of the nineties Dr. Harry Corner came to Brook House in Southgate and he also started a herd of pedigree Jerseys and he and I together started the scientific breeding of cattle. I became very interested in the subject and eventually started a herd of pedigree Shorthorns in Oxfordshire. My father died in 1932. We sold the land for building and I went back to Hill House. We just filled in the cellars and left them as they were. The stones of old Blackfriars Bridge are under the gardens of the houses which were built on the site of the house.

The Model Farm which was afterwards known as Camelot, lay on the other side of the brook in the dip. Miss Cresswell tells us that people used to retire from business and think they could make a good thing of a little farm but that they all lost money. At one time Brahminy cows were to be seen there which were of great interest to the children in the village. On the lawn in front of the house was a pair of tall pink may trees which were a sight when they were in bloom. Mr. Merrell was the first occupant I knew. His daughter married Mr. Paulin's brother. He let off the pig styes to Dan Harlow our one and only postman, an old man with a grey beard and the father of the cab proprietor in later days. One day he took nurse and me to see him feed his pigs. Later Mr. Clark, who was secretary of the Colonial Bank, took the house without the land and changed the name to Camelot. He had two sons, both of whom were much older than I was. They both went to Trinity Hall, Cambridge. James the elder became a Fellow of the College—afterwards went to the Bar and eventually was appointed legal adviser to the Minister of Agriculture. Herbert became a solicitor. The Clarks were followed by the Skeltons and then by the Stills and then came the Roberts. Mr. Roberts was born in Tasmania, came to England and went to Oxford. He became governor of the London Hospital and subsequently treasurer of St. Thomas. He had two sons, the elder was killed in the 1914 war and the younger went to Kenya.

Beyond Camelot was another small farm kept by Tom Nickels. We used to have our milk from him. He had been the conductor on the bus which ran three times a day from Winchmore Hill to Islington before the railway was made. If you wanted to go by bus you had to go to see Nickels the night before to get him to reserve a seat for you. If you did not get a seat you had to walk to Colney Hatch Station which is now named New Southgate and catch a train. In 1882 or 1883 Park Villas were built on Nickels Farm and Hounsden Road was begun as a short cul-de-sac. We then began to talk about Winchmore Hill being ruined, and that was our cry for many years.

On the left-hand side of the road a high brick wall was the boundary of Uplands garden, and extended almost as far as the meeting house. Then came an old house also enclosed by a brick wall. The grounds included an orchard bounded by a tarred wooden fence and a row of lime trees which extended as far as the Church. I saw the lime trees being lopped from my nursery window. Miss Barnes lived here. A man and his wife lived in a cottage adjoining the house and between them they looked after Miss Barnes and also the grounds. Miss Barnes also owned Hill House where her father, Robert Barnes, had lived. She belonged to a sect that had a chapel somewhere in London and she used to go there every Sunday. She died about 1904. My mother and I went to the sale of the furniture.

Then came Saint Paul's Church. This has been dealt with in a separate chapter. Then came the schools which were built in 1859. Mr. Taylor gave the land. My earliest recollection of the schools is when my mother and the other ladies gave a tea party to all the children. Unfortunately I was sent home with the nurse before the fun began. Morgan was the school master for many years and Mrs. Shears taught the infants. I knew many of the boys and girls who attended the school, Charles Brooks, Alfred Nottage Owers and many others. Concerts used to be held in the school as until the Village Hall was built in 1887 there was no other building available. Mr. Drought the vicar played the 'cello and his brother, Mr. Adolphus Drought, played the violin. Ada Burt played the piano, and, of course, we had Mr. Hawley the organist at St. Paul's, and Mr. Richard Davies gave us songs. The first public meeting of the Winchmore Hill Conservative Association was held here in July 1905. Our Member, Colonel Bowles, subsequently Sir Henry Bowles, gave us an address. At election times it was the polling booth.

Adjoining the school grounds was Grovelands. With the exception of the three cottages half-way down the hill, Taylor's woods, bounded by a hedge, extended as far as the dip. Beyond the dip was the park, also bounded by a hedge, which extended all the way to Southgate.

Miss Cresswell says the first of the cottages was a pretty house with a jessamine-covered verandah in which lived a Quaker lady who took life very seriously. She once told the doctor she had been born an adult. Arthur Partridge, who was our coachman and eventually the farm bailiff, lived here for many years. The low cottage next

The Village School prior to 1859.

door was, till 1859, the village school. Harry Cox tells us he went here to school and well remembered going up the steps. I first remember Cavil living here. He was often to be seen sitting on a chair outside the door. His two sons afterwards lived here. One of them, Long Joe, died some years ago. His brother is living there still. Partridge's widow, Mrs. Partridge, is still living in the third one. In the dip the brook from Grovelands lake runs under the road. Then came four more cottages. Brooks lived in the first one. One morning he was found drowned in the brook. His son Charlie was the first individual to come on the committee of the Conservative Association when I formed it. In the other three there were Reece, Raven and Palmer. Raven blew the organ in the Church and his wife often did odd jobs for my mother.

CHAPTER XI

THE QUAKERS

THE burial ground at the Friends' Meeting House is the Westminster Abbey of the Friends. From very early times it was used by well-known Friends' families such as the Bells, Freames, Barclays, Hoares, Hodgkins and many others. The ground, with house tenement and barn, was given to the Friends by John and Elizabeth Oakley about the year 1682. John Oakley was a Liveryman of the Merchant Taylors Company of the City of London. At the present time there are two essentials for becoming a Liveryman of the Company. You must be a Conservative in politics and you must belong to the Church of England. He married Elizabeth Hatch of Edmonton in 1672, whilst living in Westbury Street, Spitalfields. Later on he moved to Winchmore Hill where he lived for the remainder of his life. In those days it was a criminal offence to attend any place of worship other than the Church of England and Oakley had known imprisonment in Newgate and at Winchmore Hill in 1682 had his goods taken in lieu of a fine for attending a meeting at Winchmore Hill.

The first meeting of which there is any record was about the year 1662. William Brend who had suffered much for conscience sake spoke at a meeting here. George Fox is a famous name in connection with the Friends. From the year 1681 until his death in 1690 he was a frequent visitor to Winchmore Hill. Many of his friends in the City who were members of the sect lived here and in the neighbourhood. Edward and Elizabeth Man had a country house at Fords Green which is now known as Fords Grove and Fox used to often stay with them for several weeks at a time when he used to attend the meetings at Winchmore Hill and preach in the burial ground. Man was a hosier by trade and he lived in the City at the "Sign of the Golden Lyon" near Bishopsgate.

The first meeting house was built in 1688. It is not known what the building looked like or whether the roof was tiled or thatched but there is a record of Edward Man spending money to plant young trees around it. Part of the Meeting House was fitted up as a dwelling place and an outhouse was built and the widow French and her family were allowed to live there rent free. On one occasion she was urged to keep her pots and pans out of sight when people came to the meeting and to make her children keep quiet and not to make a noise by scampering up and down stairs when a meeting was on. These children had a legacy of £6 left to them by their grandmother. The Friends of the meeting had charge of it on their behalf. They therefore asked two of their members, John Freame and Thomas Gould, to take charge of it and allow them 6% per annum. These two members were the original founders of Barclays Bank. Sunday meetings were rarely held in the same place every week. More often they were held alternately with adjoining meetings. Thus members of small meetings were encouraged and strengthened by the visits of Friends from a distance.

In 1718 the meeting had so increased in numbers that the partition which had divided off what had been Widow French's living quarters was taken down. The year before this the M.M. considering the great inconvenience of the coaches coming into the yard at the Winchmore Hill Meeting House desired John Freame to get a post set up in the gateway to prevent them coming into the yard. In 1746 repairs were made to the wall of the burial ground, elm trees were cut down and the wood sold for the benefit of the meeting. David Barclays, senior and junior, Joseph Freame and Jonathan Bell contributed to the drainage of the burial ground in 1758 and in 1791 the meeting house having fallen into disrepair it was rebuilt with a tenement for the doorkeeper and a considerable addition was made to the wall of the burial ground. The list of subscriptions includes £50 each from the Samuel Hoares, senior and junior, and Isaac Walker of Arnos Grove, Southgate. This is the actual meeting house now in use rebuilt on the site of the old one.

From the commencement of the nineteenth century for a number of years the number of Friends actually residing in Winchmore Hill was extremely small and the meetings consisted chiefly of those from surrounding districts, the attraction which the Winchmore Hill Meeting House had for them being the number of eminent Friends who are buried in the burial ground. William Crouch who spent the evening of his life in Palmers Green and is known to us today for his account of the rise of Quakerism in London, together with his wife is also buried here. In 1823 Elizabeth Fry has recorded in her journal. "Since I last wrote I have attended Winchmore Hill Meeting to my satisfaction together with William Allen and my brother Samuel whose company I enjoyed."

John and Lydia Catchpool were local people who were members of the Winchmore Hill Meeting. He was a baker and his shop was what is now Chalkley's. Harry Cox tells us of a conversation he had with Mrs. Catchpool on the eve of his departure for Australia. Miss Cresswell tells us that she knew the daughter who at one time had owned the father's business but she had sold it to Burns who was also a Quaker, but she continued to live in Winchmore Hill. They kept bees and Miss Cresswell tells us how on one occasion they made the honey into mead. They evidently did not realise that it was intoxicating. Lydia, one of the sisters, took two glasses of it and woke up next morning still sitting by the kitchen fire which had gone out. She told the doctor that she had evidently been powerfully refreshed.

The ground in front of the gates is the private property of the Meeting and on one day in every year it is chained off to prevent the public obtaining a right-of-way by prescription.

When I was a small boy a good many smart weddings took place at the Meeting House. The long, oblong stone in front of the gates was then raised several inches above the level of the ground and the carriage folk used it when alighting from their carriages. Whenever I passed I invariably mounted the stone and walked along it.

On November the 9th, 1938, the Friends celebrated the 250th anniversary of their meeting. Mrs. Irene L. Edwards gave an informing and lively account of its long history. This was followed by two short representations in costume of scenes which might well have occurred in Winchmore Hill. The first one about 1662 was at Thacker's Barn, the original meeting house. It showed the meetings at which William Brent lately returned from America preached a powerful sermon. The second represented a session of the Enfield Monthly Meeting held at Winchmore Hill in 1709. Contemporary minutes of the meeting were read. Although the costumes worn by the members of the assembled company covered several periods one was carried back in imagination to the distant past.

CHAPTER XII

ST. PAUL'S CHURCH

ST. PAUL'S CHURCH was consecrated in 1827. Before then the inhabitants of Winchmore Hill had to go to Edmonton Church and were buried in the churchyard.

The nave of the Church was the same as it is now but the chancel was very shallow with a big east window of coloured glass. The manual of the organ was in the nave and was blown by hand. Before a service commenced we used to see Raven go in through a door to blow it. The walls were painted cream colour and there was no decoration. To all appearances the roof is supported by enormous oak beams, but these consist of plaster which adheres to the roof instead of supporting it and they have been painted to resemble oak. The vestry was on the site of the present lady chapel and the door was painted green. The gallery at the west end was the same as it is today and the boys from St. Paul's School used to sit up there with the schoolmaster. Harry Cox tells us the boys, including himself, did the same in his day. The altar and pulpit were given by Mrs. Todd who lived at Uplands. The pews were all high pews with doors.

Mr. Drought enlarged the chancel and the large east window was broken up to provide the glass for the two smaller windows. The large east window is in memory of Lewis and Jane Phillips of Beaulieu. The manual of the organ was also moved into the choir. He also substituted the present pews for the old high ones. Mr. Dewdney enlarged the chancel again. He built the present vestry and the lady chapel on the site of the old one. He also decorated the walls.

The Rev. T. Bissland was curate in charge from 1828 to 1834. He was followed by the Rev. E. B. Warren who was the first vicar from 1834 to 1844. The Rev. J. D.

Frost was vicar from 1844 to 1874. His two daughters went to Miss Tills' school with Miss Cresswell. His son emigrated to Australia. Then came the Rev. A. C. Drought who was vicar from 1874 to 1901. His appointment caused a long-standing joke in the village. A drought followed a frost. Mr. Drought died in 1901 and was buried in Southgate Cemetery. When I was a boy Mr. Moxon who lived in the Elms, and Mr. Hope who lived in Woodslee, Hounsden Road, and H. T. Salmon were among those who were in the choir and Mr. Moxon and Mr. Hope read the lessons. Later Mr. Richard Davies who followed us in Hill House was also in the choir. For some years Mr. Stanley Hawley was the organist. Eventually he was appointed to the staff of the Royal Academy of Music and we used to see his compositions for sale in the shops. We became very friendly with him and he was often in our house—and every Christmas Eve for several years he brought in the choir boys who sang carols and we gave them a supper. Eventually he left to go to a church in Hampstead and Mr. Davies who had by then left Winchmore Hill went into his choir. He died some years ago. Beard who worked for Wheeler and was the custodian of Memorial Terrace on Wades Hill was the verger.

In the early nineties Mr. Drought engaged a curate, the Rev. M. Thorley. He was followed by Mr. King and when Mr. Dewdney had built Holy Trinity in Green Lanes he appointed him the vicar. Mr. Dewdney was a curate in Edmonton and on Mr. Drought's death the Rector of Edmonton, who had the gift of the living, appointed Mr. Dewdney. He married the elder Miss Paulin. At first he lived in Rose Lodge, Winchmore Hill Road, now Montrose, but subsequently Mr. Paulin built the Vicarage. In 1908 reasons of health compelled him to move to Canada where eventually he became a canon. He died a few years ago. Mrs. Dewdney died a few years before him. He was followed by the Rev. E. N. Coulthard who was vicar from 1908 to 1925 and then came the Rev. R. Webb

Odell who was vicar from 1925 to 1930 when he was appointed vicar of a church in the West End of London and then came the Rev. G. H. Lancaster. He died in 1950 and has been followed by the Rev. F. Lampen the present vicar.

One of the windows was erected in "affectionate remembrance of Emma Elizabeth, wife of Samuel Sugden, who died May 24th, 1874."

Another in loving memory of Anne Marie Vivian who died November 16th, 1939; she was Mr. Sugden's daughter and the wife of Dr. Vivian.

The following are the tablets in the church:

"To the dear memory of Amelia Eliza Johnson, the much loved wife of Rev. Thomas Bissland, first minister of this chapel. She entered immortality on 26th October, 1829, in the 28th year of her age." This tablet was over our pew and as soon as I learned to read I knew her sad fate.

"Sacred to the memory of David Todd, Esquire, of Winchmore Hill. This tablet was erected as a tribute of sincere esteem, gratitude and affection and in commemoration of his meek and pious virtue."

"Sacred to the memory of Francis Maria Todd, widow of the above named David Todd, Esquire. Died May 28th, 1874, aged 86." Mrs. Todd presented the altar and pulpit to the church and also the pump to the well on the green.

"To the glory of God and in loving memory of Frances Sophia Cresswell who died December 4th, 1886, aged 67."

Mrs. Cresswell was the wife of Dr. Cresswell and the mother of Miss Cresswell.

"To the Glory of God and in memory of Sarah Drought who departed this life on Sunday, May 6th, 1888, aged 80 years." Mrs. Drought was the mother of the Rev. A. C. Drought, the vicar. "To the Glory of God and in memory of the Rev. Alfred Charles Albert Drought, for 26 years the vicar of this parish. Born 15th June, 1844, died January 29th, 1901. During his incumbency the chancel was built, the present font and organ were erected and the church was re-pewed."

"Sacred to the memory of Jehu Hatcher. Died 4th May, 1907, aged 79." Mr. Hatcher was for many years churchwarden.

"To the Glory of God and in loving memory of John W. Jackson, M.R.C.S., L.R.C.P., who practised medicine in this district from 1889-1912. He died at Mombassa, British East Africa, November 24th, 1914."

"To the Glory of God and in loving memory of Richard Trevor Vivian, Captain, R.A.M.C., killed in action at the battle of Dusailah, Mesopotamia, whilst tending the wounded of the 16a Devonshire Regiment, March 8th, 1916, aged 27." Captain Vivian was a son of Dr. Vivian.

"In loving memory of Harry Burton Emerton, M.C., Major, Royal Field Artillery, killed in action at Moeuvres, 27th September, 1918, buried at Queant."

Major Emerton was a son of Mr. Emerton.

"To the Glory of God in loving memory of Richard Thomas Vivian. The electric lighting of the chancel and chapel was installed by him, Christmas, 1922. Dr. Vivian practised medicine for many years in Winchmore Hill. In the gallery are two mural paintings placed there by the widow of Jehu Hatcher and fellow parishioners.

CHAPTER XIII

CHASE SIDE

WINCHMORE HILL ROAD was formerly named Chase Side. On the right-hand corner was the Chase Side Tavern, which has been twice rebuilt. On the last occasion it was moved further back. The original building had a portico which extended over the footpath. It was supported on two round pillars which were painted to resemble marble. The path went as far as Park House. Between the footpath and the boundaries of the gardens belonging to the houses were a series of grass plots which were kept mown by the occupiers of the houses. This made the road very attractive.

Linden Lodge, the first house past the tavern, was the residence of Mr. Thomas Page, who together with his brother, Mr. Charles Page, owned the nursery business of Carter Page. He retired in the early nineties and went to live in Devonshire. The next is "Woodbank." Mr. Adams came to live here in the eighties. Two of his sons are still living in Winchmore Hill. Then there were the two cottages which have remained unaltered. "Montrose" was formerly named "Rose Lodge" and was the residence of Mr. Charles Page. The son went to school with me at Bowhay's. He has recently left Winchmore Hill. The two white houses came next. Winchmore Villa was the residence of Mrs. Leath. She was Mr. Sugden's eldest daughter. According to the local directory the Leaths were living here in 1859.

"Chaseville" was formerly called "Chaseside House." The Thurgoods lived here. The two daughters used to come to the local dances 55 years ago. "The Ivies" has been pulled down and "Ruskin Court" has been built on the site. It had a beautiful garden which went down as far as the brook which flows at the bottom of Eversley Park Road. Mr. Mare lived here. Mrs. Mare was Mr.

Charles Morgan's sister. They left in the nineties but the son, Wilfred, stayed on in Winchmore Hill. He used to come to all the dances but unfortunately he died in the early years of this century.

"Lawrence House" used to be called "Marlborough House." The Neaves lived here. Mrs. Thomas Page was Mr. Neaves' sister. When I was in Cape Town I stayed at "Arthur's Seat Hotel" at Sea Point, which belonged to a son. "Woodbine Cottage" stands back from the road. "Park House" was the residence of Mr. Jehu Hatcher, for many years a churchwarden of St. Paul's. The son, George Hatcher, and his two sisters also used to come to the dances. George Hatcher, who was an architect, married Mr. Sewell's daughter. The Home Farm, which was a portion of the Grovelands Estate, extended from "Park House" to the cottages which are in Southgate. Joe King was the tenant for many years. The field adjoining the road and which ran up to Southgate was arable and many a time I have seen King ploughing it and subsequently reaping a harvest of corn. When King took another farm in the country Emerton took the farm. About fifteen years ago I went to see the cattle sold when the farm was sold up as the land was to be built on.

On the other side of the road the boundary of Grovelands extended right up to Southgate. As far as Jukes' house, which was in the bend of the road, there was a hedge and a belt of trees, which made the road very picturesque. Above the rise in the road was a pond on which we boys used to go to slide. "Hope House," which was the dower house of the Taylors, was a long, two-storied building. The lawn in front of the house was crescent-shaped to follow the bend in the road. A tall belt of shrubs gave privacy to the house. Mr. Jukes was the tenant. A son, Herbert, and a daughter, were about my age. The others were younger. I went to several children's parties there. Past "Hope House" the park was bounded by a wooden fence and we were able to see the deer in the park. We could also see two cedar trees at some distance from the road which marked the site of a mansion which the Taylors pulled down in order to throw the land into Grovelands.   Then came   another hedge with a belt of trees which extended all the way to Southgate.

CHAPTER XIV

COCK HILL

EVERSLEY PARK ROAD used to be called Cock Hill.
Miss Cresswell says that Cock Hill was said to be
a punning translation of Gallus or Gallow's Hill,
because one of the gibbets of Enfield Chase stood at this
spot. On the right there was a field which ran down to
the brook. Hounsden Gutter, which crosses the road,
eventually ran through part of the Stone Hall estate and
Broadfields and crosses Wades Hill. Then came the two
houses, Brookside and Woodside, one of which has been
rebuilt. Like the houses in Chase Side, these two houses
had grass plots between the boundaries of the houses and
the path and were separated from the path by posts and
chains. Behind these two houses was the Eversley Park
Estate. Further up the hill was a second entrance to
Eversley Park, with a lodge which is still standing, and
the estate went right round to Green Dragon Lane and
eventually to Wades Hill.

On the left was the Chase Side Tavern, a house in
which the original Carter Page lived, and their cottages.
Behind these was Carter Page's nursery. Carter Page was
in the Crimean War and when he left the Army he came
to Winchmore Hill and started the nursery. He took a
shop in London Wall in the City where he sold the produce
of his nursery. Then past the brook was Woodlands. Mr.
Wadman lived here. His daughter married Mr. Charles
Page, a son of Carter Page. The house was added to by
Mr. Emerton a good many years ago. Then came more
fields belonging to Mr. Sugden. His son, Mr. Charles
Sugden, lived in Ivy Lodge in the bend of the road. Then
came Dingleside, Chaseville, High Croft and Harefield.
The Burts lived in Dingleside. They had one son, Freddy,
and three daughters—May, Ada and Hetty. Ada was a
great pianist and was one of the mainsprings of our con-

certs. She married Captain Maude who was Lady Ely's private secretary. He was cousin to Cyril Maude the actor. After their father's death, the Clarks from Camelot came to live in High Croft and the Misses Sugden came to live in Harefield. Ruddock, the Congregational Minister, had lived in one of these houses previously. I must have known the sons because I told my mother that they had their clothes made by a tailor in London and I did not see why she should have mine made by a third-rate tailor in Winchmore Hill.

A builder had planned to develop the whole of the Chaseville Park Estate. When he had built the two tall white houses it was decided to build the hospital on the land adjoining. This was in the early eighties. Everybody in Winchmore Hill was convinced that we should all catch every infectious disease known to medical science. The two houses either remained empty or were let for a few shillings a week and the builders didn't build any more.

CHAPTER XV

VICARS MOOR LANE

PART of Winchmore was a moor. When the land was enclosed part of the moor was given to the Vicar of Edmonton, Winchmore Hill then being a part of the Parish of Edmonton. Hence the name Vicarsmoor.

On the right Percy Lodge was at the corner of the road. The next house was Moorslea where Mr. Watson lived. He used to drive about in a high buggy. The son went to Uppingham at the same time as my brother Cyrus. They left about the beginning of the century. The footpath from Vicarsmoor Lane to the Green is just the same today as it was 70 years ago; on the one side is the brick wall which is the boundary of Moors Lea, on the other side a wooden fence with shrubs growing on the railway bank.

Mr. Charles Morgan's father lived in a house which used to stand where the railway is now and was, of course, pulled down when the railway was built—his name appears in the 1859 Directory. He was a prominent coursing man and won the Waterloo Cup. Miss Cresswell tells us that he had a pack of 30 or 40 greyhounds and they ran in a large field adjoining the Trapgates. Sometimes they would jump the hedges and alarm passers-by. They were also exercised on the roads and did a good deal of damage. Many a small dog was worried and killed by them to say nothing of cats and poultry.

Vicarsmoor was built by Mr. Ashleigh who was the general manager of the Great Northern Railway. He lived at Roseville on the Green and built Vicarsmoor as his future home, but he died before it was completed. Mr. and Mrs. Currie lived here for some years and eventually the Burts from Dingleside. Then came Mr. Mann's house Roseneath. It was quite a small house, about the size of Drayton Villa further down the road. His son, Sir Edward

Mann, built the present house in the nineties. Mr. Mann
came from Norfolk and founded the firm of Mann Cross-
man and Paulin. One night the house was burgled and the
next morning my nurse took me to see it. Mr. Mann had
two sons and two daughters. One daughter married Mr.
Paulin, and the other, Miss Julia, was totally blind. When
they were small children they were playing together and
her brother Edward accidentally poked a pair of scissors
into one of her eyes.

Rose Cottage was very picturesque. Miss Cresswell
called it a dear old place—roofed with shingle tiles, red-
brown and mossy. The boundary of the road was a brick
wall and a line of trees. On one side of the house was a
lawn with a vegetable garden beyond. There was also
stabling and a coach house. Tom Hood, the poet, lived
here from 1829 to 1832. Later the back of the house was
added to. The dining room and the drawing room were
modern. When Mr. Drought came to live here the old
dining room became his study. The first people I remember living here were the Warners. They had moved from
the Shrubbery in Green Lanes. Mr. Warner was a keen
cricketer and played in the village team along with James
Waters, Charles Sugden and others. His son died just as
he was growing up and as they were Quakers he is buried
in the Quaker Burial Ground.

When the Warners left Mr. Drought came to live here
and many happy hours I spent in the house. After Mr.
Drought's death Miss Julia Mann took it and when she
left the district Mr. Charles Morgan's widow came to live
here.

Then came Pritchett Terrace and Hescott Terrace.
Just before you came to Pritchett Terrace there was the
Vicars Well. Before the water was laid on to the houses
they used to get water from this well. Harry Cox used to
fetch water from here. Eventually a baby's dead body was
found in the well. The individual who put it there was
never found but the well was closed. Mrs. Belcher, an
old lady who lived in the first house, had a number of

Rose Cottage.

white Pomeranians which she used to take out walking with her. Whenever she met us out with our nurse she used to speak to us. The end of Hescott Terrace was only a few feet from Green Lanes.

On the left-hand side of the road was Beaumont Lodge. This was formerly the residence of John Wade, of whom Harry Cox tells us so much and after whom Wades Hill is named. The house was added to after Mr. Wade's time. Mr. Mann's eldest son lived here for a short time but he soon left the district. Eventually the name of the house was changed to Avondale and it became a boarding school for girls. They used to come to church on a Sunday. Next came a furniture shop belonging to Beadle. I used to see rolls of oilcloth outside the shop leaning against the wall. One morning when the nurse came to get me up she told me there had been a fire at Beadle's shop and that it had been burnt out. So after breakfast she took me to see the ruins. Beadle never rebuilt the shop nor resumed his business. On the site of the shop he built the three villas now named Braeside, Burnham and Royston, and on the opposite side of the road he built a house for himself which he called Herbert Lodge.

Mr. Drought then moved from Glenwood House in Wades Hill to the one next the Baptist Chapel. Eventually he bought a tricycle which Mr. Paulin allowed him to keep in his coachhouse. One day when I was about seventeen he asked me if I would go for a ride with him. I had a bicycle. That was the first of many most enjoyable rides I had with him in my school holidays and later in the Cambridge vacations. Sometimes we went out two and even three times a week. We explored all the country round St. Albans, Hertford, Ware, Epping, etc., etc. Many times we had tea in the "Dimsdale Arms," in Hertford.

For many years Beadle's son, Joe Beadle, and H. T. Salmon were our representatives on the Local Board and also on the Guardians, and later on the District Council. There were no elections because nobody else wanted the job. They were both keen Conservatives and it was not till Skelton came to Camelot that politics were introduced into local affairs.

The Baptist Chapel was founded by the Udalls who dealt in smuggled goods on week-days and went to church on Sundays. The Minister was an old man who lived in a cottage in Middle Lane. One Sunday he did not turn up so the deacons went to look for him. They found him hoeing potatoes—he had forgotten it was Sunday. The chapel was rebuilt in 1888.

Mr. Paton lived in Holmwood. He was cousin to William Walker of Avondale in Hoppers Road. Mrs. Paton was Mr. Charles Morgan's eldest daughter. Their son who I knew as quite a small boy, years younger than me is a Colonel in the Army. There was also a younger sister, Madge Paton.

Then came the four cottages North Row. Arlow's cowman lived in the first one. Then came Iver Jasmine Cottage, Verandor Cottage and Monkton Lodge. Harry Cox lived in Jasmine Cottage. The railway and the goods yard are just as they were when I was a boy. Then came five houses and then Suburban House. Miss Cresswell tells us that two brothers, Charles and William Brett, lived here. They were a remarkable couple. They were very strict Quakers and were the only two brothers who wore the Quaker garb. They wore long dark brown coats with knee breeches, white stockings, buckled shoes and shovel hats. They were formerly hardware merchants in Birmingham. They both left all their money to their cook who married Mr. Arlow, no relation to the Arlow who had previously lived in Highfield Park. Suburban House had a good deal of land attached to it. The boundaries were Vicarsmoor Lane, Hagfields Footpath and Green Dragon Lane. Mr. Arlow kept Jersey cows.

Hagfields Footpath led from Vicars Moor Lane to Green Dragon Lane. Miss Cresswell tells us that at the junction with Green Dragon Lane there used to be an inn "The Retreat." If you wanted to walk to Enfield the shortest way was along this path, and then across Green Dragon Lane. Then there was another path across Pike's farm and then there was a third path leading down to the New River. You then followed the path along the bank of the river. You had Mr. Twells's estate on your right—this is now the Enfield Park—and you came out at the foot of Windmill Hill.

Then came Drayton Villa. There was a small farm-yard and buildings at the rear. A field belonging to it ran along Hagfields Footpath. Mr. Booth, the founder of Booths Gin, lived here and Mrs. Booth is in the 1859 Directory. In the early eighties a family named Bullock lived here and the son went to Enfield Grammar School at the same time as Mr. Jack Walker. A few yards further on was Green Lanes.

CHAPTER XVI

MIDDLE LANE

WHAT is now Station Road was officially known as Middle Lane, but some people used to call it Waterses Lane, because James Waters had a grocer's shop in it. On the right, fields swept all the way down from the railway line to Green Lanes, or what is now the Broadway. The field adjoining the line was occupied by Lincoln, one of our two cab proprietors. In the middle of the field was a shed in which he kept his horses and his cab. We often heard Mrs. Houlder speaking of her husband arriving home (they lived on the site of Duncan Court) in Lincoln's cab. He was on the Common Council in the City and was a Liveryman of two or three Companies and so frequently had late nights. The two cabs, Lincoln's and Harlow's, when not engaged were generally to be seen standing outside the railway station.

Adjoining the "Queen's Head" was a small grocer's shop with a cottage next door. The shop had originally belonged to James Waters' father and the family lived in the cottage. Now the son had the shop. He was a well-known figure in Winchmore Hill. We used to see him attired in a clean white apron and a bowler hat, with a basket under his arm, delivering groceries to his customers. He wore mutton-chop whiskers which have now gone out of fashion. Mrs. Waters used to make jams and pickles which he used to sell. His great interest in life was cricket and he was Winchmore Hill's best player. Many years later he moved across the road to what is now Skinner's shop. He lived in retirement for a good many years and died a few years ago well up in the nineties.

The "Queen's Head" is a very old inn. It has been rebuilt in recent years. Dick Turpin used to lie up here. He had scouts in the main road through Edmonton and Tottenham, and when they saw anybody coming along who was worthy of his attention they used to come to tell Dick, who would then go out to meet them. Garner kept it and then James Barnes took it. He had been our coachman. When I was about five years old he taught me to ride a pony. I have a vivid recollection of the first time I was put on the pony's back. It was in the yard at Hill House. I told the pony to gee up, and James, as we used to call him, told me to keep quiet. We walked to the bottom of Church Hill and then trotted all the way back again, poor James running beside the pony holding the rein and at the same time teaching me how to rise in the stirrups. When this had been repeated six or eight times my lesson for the day was finished. After some weeks of this, James rode a horse and had my pony on a leading rein. It was a good long time before the leading rein was dispensed with. James Barnes' son now has the inn.

There were also other cottages. Mrs. Jordan, who took in washing, lived in one, and Mrs. Seal, who did mangling, lived in the other. We often used to take the washing to her, to be mangled, in the governess's cart, which the French governess usually drove. On one occasion, when we were stationary outside Mrs. Seal's, a cart came along and ripped off our mudguard. Mrs. Seal had an old wooden box mangle. When she died my mother bought it and we used it for many years. My brother has it now, a relic of old Winchmore Hill. Then came an old wooden stable and a shed in which Harlow, the other cab proprietor, a son of Dan Harlow, the old postman, kept his horses and cab.

Opposite Herbert Lodge was a footpath across the field leading to Compton Road. This path was bordered by a row of elm trees, of which one is still standing. When I was a boy the Houlders were my principal friends and this footpath was the shortest cut to their house on the site of Duncan Court. I therefore frequented it pretty often.

Below the railway station on the other side of the

Holly Cottage and the Shop, once Chalkley's, in Middle Lane.

road is Holly Cottage. In the past the Villiers used to live here. Later on, the Binsteads had both the house and the adjoining shop, now Skinners. Mrs. Binstead was a Udall — sister to Mrs. Child. They were bakers and confectioners. Miss Cresswell tells us how, as a child, she used to go there to buy cakes. She also describes the garden, which was always gay with flowers, and a high rockery on which there was a collection of ferns. Binstead sold the business to Stern who took over the shop, but the Binsteads retained Holly Cottage where they lived in retirement for many years. Many a time I have seen Mr. Binstead working in the garden. Stern sold the business to Mr. Chalkley's grandfather about 1880 or soon after. He used a pony and trap for delivering the bread, and many a time I saw Mr. Chalkley's father, then a boy of nine or ten, helping with the delivery. Now Chalkleys have a smart motor van. The other day I shook hands with Mr. Chalkley's small daughter, so I have now known four generations of the family. Another baker, Goldsworthy, had the old wooden shop in Hoppers Road. He was also a corn merchant. We used to go there with our governess to buy the food for our fowls. Goldsworthy had a long red beard. When he died, Chalkley bought his business and gave up the shop in Middle Lane which was taken by Press as a newsagent's. Press had two sons who were identically alike. Later on, Fred came to us as a groom; his brother went in a similar capacity to Mr. Paulin. On weekdays, when they were in their stable clothes, I could tell which was which since the clothes were of different materials, but when I met either of them on a Sunday, when they were dressed in the private clothes, I had to ask him which of the two he was. Fred subsequently married the daughter of the former proprietor of the "Salisbury" and who then owned the house. A few years ago Fred dropped down dead in the Broadway. When Fred's father died, Waters took the shop and had it for his grocery business, and when he retired Skinner took it.

A wooden fence was the boundary of Mr. Mann's Roseneath estate. A paddock between the gardens and the road was occupied by the Winchmore Hill Tennis Club. The entrance was a gate adjoining the shop. In those days the club was very exclusive. I remember G. H. was so elated at having been admitted a member that one might have almost imagined he had become a member of White's Club. The house which is now called Herbert Lodge was Miss MacLaurin's school. Below this was a field which extended all the way to Green Lanes without a house on it. I often played cricket in this field with the Houlders and other boys. At the junction of Middle Lane with Green Lanes there was a triangular piece of turf with a signpost in the centre.

CHAPTER XVII

BACK LANE

COMPTON ROAD used to be called Back Lane and once we got away from the railway it was a very pretty country lane. On the right was Holly Lodge. It was the residence of Mr. Claringbull who was the engineer in charge of the making of the railway from Wood Green to Enfield.

Across the railway bridge was the Congregational Church. This was not the original building. It is not known when the Church was founded but it was prior to 1750, as at that date there was a little wooden conventicle at the entrance to the wood in the cul-de-sac which is now part of the Broad Walk. When the building was pulled down to make way for Woodside Cottages, a number of bones were dug up which showed that there had been burials there. When Clark, our gardener, left us, he went to live in one of the cottages and he told me that a part of his cottage had evidently come out of a church. The lease of the land on which the conventicle stood expired in June, 1841, and an attempt to buy the land was unsuccessful. The Church, however, secured the gift of a plot of land in Hoppers Road on the site of the present skew bridge. It was next to Trois Vase House, the original home of the Cresswells. There was also room to build a school behind the Church. A white brick chapel was built with some pretensions to ecclesiastical design. The first minister to be called to the Hoppers Road Chapel was the Rev. J. Charles Richards who commenced his ministry in 1846. Twenty years later in 1866, the Great Northern Railway served a notice that the land on which the Church stood would be required for the new line. They paid £2,750 for the land and the building. A temporary chapel was then secured, but where it was is not known now and the present Church was opened in October, 1874. The new schoolroom was built in 1881 and the Church was extended, and the chancel or organ loft were added in 1914. The Scout Troop was started in 1917. The Rev. J. B. Ruddock became the Minister in 1877 and left to go to Australia in 1886. He was followed by the Rev. John Jermyn who remained for 12 fairly uneventful years. Then came the Rev. Arthur Jarvis who was Minister for 21 years. He was followed by the Rev. Percy Martin, and in 1937 the Rev. W. A. Oyler-Waterhouse came and he is still the Minister.

Once past the Church we came to the boundary of the Highfield Park estate which consisted of a brick wall and a belt of trees which shaded the road. Near the junction with Green Lanes were two houses, Clock House and Windermere. Jardine, a Frenchman, lived in the Clock House. In his time it was burnt out. It was rebuilt and Captain Lichfield came to live there. The son, Charlie Lichfield, was at Bowhay's School with me. Mr. and Mrs. Newman lived in Windermere and they were followed by Mr. and Mrs. Hoskins whose daughter used to come to the dances.

On the left-hand side of the road fields extended from Hoppers Road to Green Lanes—one, of course, being intersected by the railway. Across the other was a pathway leading to Middle Lane. There was a grass verge and a hedge all along this side of the road except for the railway bridge and I have gathered blackberries here.

CHAPTER XVIII

MORTIBOYS LANE

WE always called Fords Grove Mortiboy's Lane. On the right Mortiboy's farm extended from the New River to Firs Lane. One field separated the farm buildings from the river. Miss Cresswell calls the house an ancient cottage with its diamond-paned leaded windows and mossy roof of shingle tiles, every shade of rich red and brown, bright near the eaves with yellow patches of poor man's pepper, light green mosses and huge rosettes of house leeks. Captain Tills had lived there. Miss Cresswell describes him as a sweet-faced little old sailor man with a fresh colour and silver hair and whiskers, and his wife as a tall pleasant old lady who might have stepped out of a picture. Captain Tills had been in the Battle of Trafalgar. He had one son and two daughters. His means would not allow the son to be an officer so he enlisted in the Army as a private and was killed in the seige of Delhi in the Indian Mutiny. Captain Tills died in the early sixties. His wife and one daughter died soon after. Charlotte then had to do something. Mrs. Todd of Uplands had made it possible for her to attend a School of Art in London and twice a week she went up and returned by omnibus. Now, however, she decided to start a school for girls. Miss Cresswell says she went to the school when she was ten years old. The Cresswells then lived at the house Trois Vases in Hoppers Road where the railway bridge is now. Miss Cresswell took a short cut by going through the park of Highfield. Two daughters of Mr. Frost, the vicar, and also some other girls attended the school. Subsequently Miss Tills moved her school to one of the houses on the Green, now a shop, and the old cottage was taken by Mortiboy, and she says it became very different from what it had been with the old furniture, china, silver and curios.

Mortiboy kept a herd of cows and supplied everybody in the district with milk. After his death his son had the business and in the end sold it to Nix.

On the left-hand side of the lane was the large, old, red brick house, Fords Grove, in which Mr. Busk lived. His land also extended to Firs Lane. Mortiboy rented the land and grazed his cows on it.

According to the 1859 directory there were three other houses in Fords Grove occupied by Matthew Costin, John Farrin and John Simmons. George Fox used often to stay with friends who had a house in Fords Grove, when he used to attend the meetings and preach in the burial ground of the Quakers' meeting house. These houses were evidently pulled down and the land thrown into the Fords Grove property. Eventually, Mr. Paulin bought a good deal of the land and Miss Paulin has let it to the Cricket Club.

On both sides of the lane there were rows of trees which overhung the road and made it a very pretty lane. At the end of the lane on the left-hand side was a long pond which extended round the corner into Firs Lane. We often used to come here to fish for minnows. I am afraid our French governess must have got very tired standing there while we fished.

CHAPTER XIX

JORDAN'S LANE

JORDAN'S LANE is now called Farm Road. On the right was Jordan's farm, the land of which extended all the way to Firs Lane. The farmyard came right up to the New River. Below the farm buildings was a footpath from Jordan's Lane to Highfield Row. On the other side of the lane was Mortiboy's farm which also extended as far as Firs Lane. There were many trees on both sides of the lane which made a very pretty effect. There were also many wild flowers that grew on both banks.

CHAPTER XX

HIGHFIELD ROAD

HIGHFIELD ROAD used to be called Highfield Row. Beyond the New River bridge on the right was a row of cottages. The building line was very irregular and they did not all face exactly the same way. The people got their water by dipping a bucket in the New River and obviously did not pay any water rate. The inn was the "Orange Tree." Miss Cresswell was evidently rather taken with it. It had a round bow window with small panes and there were benches in the porch. The landlord was Davis and later Abbott. In recent years it was pulled down and rebuilt. Separated from the "Orange Tree" by one cottage there was originally another public house, the "Moulder's Arms," a mere black wooden cottage. The licensee was Hunt, a brickmoulder. Hence the name. It protruded far beyond the irregular building line in Highfield Row and the site is now part of the road. On the other side of the road was a flowing brook.

Old Moore, the first gardener we had at Hill House, lived in Highfield Row. George Kirby kept a shop and he was the lamp-lighter, turning on and turning off the street lamps with a pole. Marriage, a builder, built five cottages in Highfield Row and his son kept a shop. The son subsequently came on the Committee of the Winchmore Hill Conservative Association. Mrs. Woodcock took in washing. Early in the nineties some of the old ladies in Highfield Row told Mr. Drought that it was too far for them to walk to St. Paul's Church; he therefore built the corrugated iron chapel near the footpath that goes from Highfield Row to Jordan's Lane.

Once past the cottages there were green fields on both sides of the lane to the junction with Firs Lane. Halfway along was a small pond on the left. I have fished in it for minnows. At the junction with Firs Lane on the right was a cottage standing well back from the road. Mrs. Pickering lived here and took in washing.

CHAPTER XXI

BARROWELL GREEN

BARROWELL GREEN was a lane that ran parallel to Highfield Road and Hedge Lane. The pumping station adjoining the New River was not erected till the early eighties. There was one small house close to the New River on the left and a row of cottages at the further end on the right. Otherwise it was fields all the way on both sides of the lane. Those on the right were part of Bunce's Farm and those on the left were part of Firs Farm.

CHAPTER XXII

HEDGE LANE

HEDGE LANE had fields all the way on either side except for Mr. Charles Morgan's house on the right at the junction with Green Lanes and Huxley Farm which was half-way down on the left. The farm belonged to Mr. Booth Smith, otherwise Gentleman Smith, to distinguish him from Pop Smith of Oak Tree Villa, the pawnbroker. His daughter used to come to our dances.

Eventually the lane joined up with Silver Street, Edmonton. Until the two parishes were separated Winchmore Hill was part of the parish of Edmonton. Edmonton used to be a good residential neighbourhood. The Great Eastern Railway was the first one to institute cheap workmen's fares and then both Edmonton and Tottenham became working-class districts. I remember seeing about the last of the red brick gentlemen's houses being pulled down to make way for workmen's dwellings. Down to the Redistribution Act of 1918, Edmonton and Winchmore Hill were both included in the Enfield Parliamentary Division, and when I was Treasurer for the Division I had a good deal to do with Edmonton.

CHAPTER XXIII

FIRS LANE

FIRS LANE runs from Hedge Lane to Green Lanes (past the "Green Dragon"). With the exception of two farms and a few cottages there were fields all the way to the bridge across the New River. When Winchmore Hill was being built up I often felt I wanted a whiff of the country so I used to go to Firs Lane where not a single house was to be seen. There were six cottages on the left-hand side and one on the right. Bunce had the land on both sides of the road, that on the left extending to Green Lanes. His farm buildings were on the right but he also had a barn on the opposite side of the road. When we were passing there about 70 years ago we saw women tying up rhubarb into bundles to go to market. A cousin of Bunce's was Chairman of the Chase and Bulls

Bunce's Farm, Firs Lane.

Conservative Association in Enfield and as Treasurer I had a good deal to do with him. On the opposite side of the road at the junction with Barrowell Green was Firs Farm. Kurzon had it. Then we passed Highfield Row and Jordans Lane and came to the junction with Mortiboy's Lane. On the right was a footpath across a field which led to the Hyde in Edmonton. This footpath used to be used by those from Winchmore Hill and Southgate who went to Edmonton Church. Further on was a road which was parallel with the footpath. The junction of this road with Firs Lane was for some reason or other called Jews Corner. On the other side of the river was River Bank, a house that stood well back from the road. A Frenchman of the name of Bresand lived here. He evidently had a business in London. He used to go to and fro every day accompanied by his lady secretary who lived in the thatched cottage at Palmers Green. Then came two cottages, Gibraltar Cottages at the junction with Bush Hill. Fuller and Anderson lived here. They had greenhouses in their gardens and grew flowers to sell.

On the left was the park attached to Fords Grove which extended to the New River. On the other side of the river was Beaulieu which was bounded by Bush Hill and Green Lanes. There was a barred fence and a plantation of trees which made the road very picturesque. Adjoining the river was a cottage for one of the gardeners.

Firs Lane. Firs Farm on right.

CHAPTER XXIV

GREEN DRAGON LANE

GREEN DRAGON LANE took its name from the Green Dragon which originally stood at the junction of the lane with Bush Hill. About 1780 a highwayman was hanged in front of the inn because of a crime he had committeed in the neighbourhood. About 1800 the inn was moved to its present site.

On the right hand side of the lane was Pike's Farm which extended as far as the railway line. Salmon's Brook ran through the farm roughly parallel with the road and then went under Bush Hill and the New River. It passes Bury Street, widening out into the Wash of Edmonton and finally entering the River Lea. Mr. Pike went in extensively for fruit growing and most of the land between the road and the brook was orchards. Across the brook were grass fields with the farm buildings on the top of the hill. Opposite Hagfields path was a path across the farm. You went first downhill through orchards. You then crossed the brook by a wooden bridge and then went through the grass fields. This brought you to a lane which you crossed and entered another path which went down to the New River. You then followed the river bank with Mr. Twells's estate, which is now Enfield's Park, on your right and this brought you out at the bottom of Windmill Hill. When we wanted to walk to Enfield this was the way we always went. Beyond the railway was Filcap Farm. Perkins had the farm and then later on Mr. Gurlitt who lived in "The Shrubbery" in Green Lanes took it. The farm buildings were about opposite the Chase. It was originally intended to build the hospital on this side of the road but the price which was asked for the land was too much so it was eventually built on its present site, the land being purchased from Mr. Sugden.

On the left, with the exception of one row of cottages, there were fields all the way until we came to three houses adjoining Hagfields Path. Mr. and Mrs. Dale lived in the end one. Mrs. Dale was very clever and painted pictures. They had a son Joey and a daughter Mary. Joey was a year or two older than me. They had a donkey. Joey and I often used to ride together on the donkey, bare backed. Also they often used to bring the donkey to graze in our orchard. The fields of Suburban House extended from the path to the railway line, those of the Chase to Wades Hill and the Eversley Park Estate stretched from Wades Hill to Eversley Park Road, the stables being about halfway.

The World's End, a narrow lane, was an extension of Green Dragon Lane. There were fields on both sides with a farm house and farm buildings halfway along on the right. The lane ended in a cul-de-sac with a gate leading into a field and on the left was a path across a field which led into Bramley Road near the bottom of Slades Hill. The World's End was a favourite walk of our Nurse's and we children took the name quite literally and were much puzzled when we saw green fields beyond the end of the world.

CHAPTER XXV

BUSH HILL

GREEN LANES extends past the "Green Dragon" as far as Green Dragon Lane. The lane got its name because the inn used to stand on the corner of the lane till it was moved to the present site soon after 1800. A highwayman was hanged opposite the inn and the gibbet was left standing there so the inn was moved. In the same way a gibbet used to stand on Cock Hill and the name Cock was said to be a Punning translation of Gallus or Gallows.

On the right was the black-tarred fence of Beaulieu where Mr. Phillips lived. He died in 1892. Behind the fence was a fine belt of trees which overhung the road and made it a very pretty spot. Then came Firs Lane. In the further corner were two cottages, Gilbraltar Cottages. Fuller and Anderson lived here. They had greenhouses behind the cottages and sold flowers. Then came some vacant land which extended as far as the boundary of the Bush Hill House Estate. A new road, Ridge Avenue, has recently been made through the land and is now the main road to Enfield. It is a shorter road and saves climbing up the hill.

On the left-hand side was the "Green Dragon" which was quite a small building compared with the present erection. On top of the front wall was a large painting of a Green Dragon. Then came a few cottages and then a field which extended as far as Green Dragon Lane.

Beyond the lane the road was Bush Hill. Prior to 1786 the dip in the road was much deeper than it is today. Salmons Brook, which now runs under the road, ran over it. On the right, all the way up to the top of the hill, was an oak fence which was the boundary of the Bush Hill House Estate. The fine trees on the estate made this a very pretty lane.

A few yards inside the fence is a long embankment. The New River flows along it. Originally the river was carried over a wooden aqueduct which was lined with zinc. The Gordon Riots took place in 1780. Lord George Gordon had much to do with firing the tempers of the rioters. His father had a house in Enfield where Gordon Hill now stands. He therefore knew the district well. The intention of the rioters was to deprive London of its water supply by destroying the aqueduct. To guard against this two regiments of soldiers were quartered in Southgate. Subsequently it was decided to substitute the present embankment for the aqueduct. Bush Hill House is at the top of the hill. Sir Hugh Myddleton lived here when he was constructing the New River. The Honourable Samuel Cunard lived here at the time of the 1859 directory. In my time it was Mr. Barry. They came to St. Paul's Church. His son, Fred Barry, married and came to live at The Laurels in Church Hill, when the Manns moved to Roseneath. He afterwards moved to Enfield. Bush Hill House is now called Halliwick and is a home for girls.

On the left, Pike's farm, which was all planted with fruit trees, extended as far as Salmon's Brook; beyond the brook were the fields attached to Elmscott, a large house also on the top of the hill. Over the brook is an arch which supported the piers of the wooden aqueduct which carried the New River. The arch bears an inscription that it was rebuilt in 1682 when Henry Earl of Clarendon was Governor of the New River Company.

On the top of the hill is a footpath which used to be known as the Poets' Walk. The road to Enfield here makes a big bend and the footpath is a short cut. The nearest way to Enfield was to cross Pike's fields and along the bank of the New River, but we did not care to go this way after dark. We might have fallen into the river, so at night we always went via Bush Hill.

CHAPTER XXVI

CONSERVATIVE ASSOCIATION

MY first introduction to politics was about 1889. Down to 1918 we were part of the Enfield Division of Middlesex. A by-election was caused by our member, Viscount Folkestone, succeeding to the peerage on the death of his father, the Earl of Radnor—we went to the Village Hall to hear an address by Colonel Henry Bowles, later Sir Henry Bowles, Bart., the Conservative Candidate. Both he and his supporters wore flaming scarlet ties, red being the Conservative colour throughout Middlesex. Colonel Bowles won hands down.

In 1904 and 1905 a Conservative government under Mr. Balfour was in power; the Opposition were the Liberals under Sir Henry Campbell Bannerman. The Conservatives were losing all the by-elections. In Winchmore Hill we had not had a Conservative Association for ages—I felt very strongly that we ought to have one, but I found everybody very apathetic, and in spite of many efforts I was unable to get anyone to make a move. I therefore decided that I must start a Conservative Association myself. The first thing to be done was to form a Committee and to get people to come on. I went first to Charlie Brooks. He and I had been boys together. He was gardener to the Stills at Camelot. He was delighted to come on. I then got Alfred Nottage. He used to bring Charlie Letchfield to school at Bowhays—his mother used to come to do our washing. One day when I was about seven I was lying on the sofa feeling very seedy when my mother noticed some spots on my face. She fetched Mrs. Nottage who diagnosed measles. Nottage worked at Carter Page's Nursery. He gladly came in and later on brought in Mr. Jones, his foreman. I then got Bennington, who drove a horse and cart for Gabriel, the

Downes' predecessor and finally I got Charlie Finch who did jobbing work. All of these were keen Conservatives and hard workers in the cause.

If our association was to be truly democratic it was essential that I should get the other sections of the community to come in. There were the newcomers who lived in the houses which had been recently erected in Compton Road and in Elm Park Road on the Beaulieu estate. Unfortunately I did not know a single one of them even by sight. I therefore went to the tradespepole who come into personal contact with their customers and asked them to put me on to some. They recommended Mr. Arthur Willis, afterwards Colonel Willis, Mr. A. B. Vialou and Mr. Edward Linstead. I went to see Willis and asked him to be the Chairman of the Committee and asked Vialou and Linstead to come on. They all three gladly accepted. Vialou did valuable work for the Enfield Division, till he moved from the district and Willis and Linstead subsequently became Chairmen of the Wood Green Division. Dunnett, Marriage, David Bonner and James Fossey completed the numbers. We held our Committee meetings in a room over Palmer's Shop—now Guys. We held a public meeting one Saturday afternoon in St. Paul's school when our member, Colonel Bowles, addressed us.

Then came the General Election in January, 1906. Mr. Harry Godwin who acted as Col. Bowles' election agent asked me to be sub-Agent for Winchmore Hill. We had our committee room in a room behind Salmon's shop. We had six hundred and seventy four electors on the register. Our Committee were most enthusiastic, they not only canvassed Winchmore Hill but also a good part of Edmonton. I was present at the counting of the votes in the Athenæum in Enfield. Mr. James Branch, the Radical candidate won by a large majority. We were all much amused when Mr. Branch as soon as the returning officer had announced the result, dropped on his knees and said his prayers. We set to work and got members for our association. We held a good many meetings in the conservatory at Highfield House, by kind permission of Mr. Wilkinson. I also thought we should have a Habitation of the Primrose League for the ladies. Mrs. Lindsay Blee, of Enfield, kindly came over. We held an inaugural meeting in Mr. Wilkinson's conservatory and founded the Lansdowne Habitation, of which Mrs. Wilkinson became the Secretary. A couple of years later I was appointed Treasurer for the Enfield Division. It was considered desirable that the Treasurer should be an impartial individual, so I was bidden to sever my connection with the Winchmore Hill Association. In the General Election of January, 1910, our Candidate was Mr. Pretyman Newman who won by a handsome majority. On this occasion Mr. Branch did not say his prayers. He accused Mr. Newman of telling lies.

CHAPTER XXVII

SOCIAL EVENTS

THE great day in Winchmore Hill was the Annual Flower Show, which was held in the second week in July. The show was held at Broadfields, The Elms, Uplands, The Chase, Roseneath and Suburban House. A large marquee was erected in the grounds and the exhibits of flowers, vegetables and fruit were placed in it. It was a great day—we met everyone we knew there. The last show was in 1907. We were unable to hold any more after that date because almost all the people in the large houses with large grounds had left the district and there was nowhere to hold the show, in addition to which these people were the principal exhibitors. The last show was held at Suburban House, Mr. Arlow's.

During the Boer War in 1900 we wanted to raise some funds for the Red Cross. We all decorated our carriages with flowers, and those who were to be the occupants dressed themselves in fancy clothes. We had a pair of cream coloured ponies with white tails which reached to their heels. One day when we were on a tour we drove into a town. Sanger's Circus was expected and the pavements were lined with people waiting to welcome them. When they saw our ponies they thought we were the vanguard of the circus and they all raised loud cheers. Cuthbert's, the nurserymen of Southgate, decorated the carriage very nicely for us. My two young brothers wore some Louis XIV dresses which we had worn at two fancy dress dances many years before and Arthur Partridge dressed as Napoleon occupied the dicky. We got our friends to form a squad of Australian Cavalry to form an escort. We hired the uniforms, and in addition to our own horses hired some from the livery stables. My own horse was given to someone else and I had to have one of the

Our Carriage in the procession for the **Red Cross.**

carriage horses. I was afraid the horse would be frightened of the lance I carried but my fears were unfounded. The procession went down Vicarsmoor Lane. Mr. Drought was looking out for us. Eventually we got to Southgate and came home along Chase Side. There were good crowds of people all along the route and several people also in fancy dress took their offerings. We collected six hundred pounds.

About 1890 the Alexandra Palace gave some very good presentations of the Fall of Pompeii. A stage with suitable scenery was erected on the island in the lake. After a lot of dances some rockets suddenly went up. They were the beginning of a fine display of fireworks, which represented the eruption of Vesuvius. When the rockets went up all the actors and actresses fled in terror. The shows were very well patronized.

In the eighties Queen Victoria opened Epping Forest to the public. The following day we went there and saw the platforms which had been erected for the ceremony.

Every August Bank Holiday there was a horse show at Waltham Cross. For several years I was on the Committee. For those who wanted to hunt there were the Enfield Chase Staghounds.

Dances were got up in the Village Hall which has since disappeared. They were well attended. The first I went to was in 1892. When I was six years old I attended dancing classes which were held by Miss Chambers who had a school for girls in Windmill Hill, Enfield, below the railway station. The classes were held in a large hall part of the school by the church. The dancing master provided the music by playing a violin.

The roads to Hatfield and Hertford and the country between them were beautiful. In the days of horses this was about the limit of our drives. When cars came along we were able to go much further afield.

I have seen Winchmore Hill grow from a village amidst the fields to be part of London. The railway had only been opened seven years before I first knew the village. The Post Office was in the wooden building across the green now occupied by Stevens and Co. Only the large houses had water laid on. Other people got their water from pumps and wells. The roads had no lights. We had to go to Southgate for a good deal of our shopping and if we mentioned Winchmore Hill to anybody they had never heard of the place. Now it is merely a part of the great town of London.